Love of the Game

MICKEY WHELAN

WITH BRIAN BARRY

www.**HERO**BOOKS.digital

HEROBOOKS

PUBLISHED BY HERO BOOKS
1 WOODVILLE GREEN
LUCAN
CO. DUBLIN
IRELAND

Hero Books is an imprint of Umbrella Publishing
First Published 2022
Copyright © Mickey Whelan and Brian Barry 2022
All rights reserved

ISBN 9781910827352

Cover design and formatting: jessica@viitaladesign.com
Ebook formatting: www.ebooklaunch.com
Photographs: Sportsfile and the Whelan family collection

Dedication

In memory of my beloved Irene

« ACKNOWLEDGEMENTS »

MY MOTHER COLLEEN spent her lifetime caring for her children and her husband; and my dad Francis spent his lifetime working hard, so that our family could have a decent life. My dad was a boilermaker by trade. He was a foreman on the building of the first power stations across the country in the early 50s.

This meant that he travelled a lot. While he was working on the nearby power stations, such as the Pigeon House station in Dublin, or in Allenwood, Portarlington and Ferbane, he could drive back home at the end of each day. But when he was working in Bellacorick in Mayo, or in Cork, he only came home at weekends. That was difficult on my mother and for us children.

The plus side for the five of us - myself, Frances, Ann, Joan and Matthew - was that our mam was always there for us when we needed her. However, it also meant that I had a lot of shopping and child-minding to do as I got older. I can recall one frightening shopping experience that I will take to the grave with me.

I was minding one of my siblings in a pram, when my mam asked me to get a few messages in the shops. I headed off with the child in the pram, and the dog alongside. I got the messages and sauntered homeward, but just as I neared our house I noticed the dog was missing. The dog who never left my side.

THE BABY??

I ran faster than I ever ran in my life back to the shop, and found the dog alongside the pram. He was wagging his tail while the baby lay sleeping in the pram, as people were going in and out of the shop. What made the whole experience so frightening was that a baby was stolen from a pram belonging to a newspaper seller in O'Connell Street some weeks before.

MY SIBLINGS AND I have so much to be grateful for, and we have our mother and dad to thank especially for fostering in each one of us a love for sport. Frances, Ann and Joan, all loved competing as much as I did, although Joan found hurling a little bit too rough and concentrated on tennis and rounders as a young girl. Frances and Ann met with success on the GAA field, but the youngest in our family, Matthew, who was an outstanding athlete, sought to forge a career in the League of Ireland.

The sporting gene was alive and thriving in the Whelan household.

TO MY FAMILY – Cormac, Shane, Michelle, Colleen and Emma - I thank you all for your kindness to me. I am very happy to see the way you support each other as you progress through life, and how our family was there for Michelle when she tragically lost her loving husband Mark at such a young age.

Your partners Maria, Mary Rose and Paul, like Mark, have enriched our family. I am also very happy to see my grandchildren grow and prosper through the different stages in their lives.

I know that you will always watch out for each other.

I AM VERY mindful of three primary schoolteachers, who played a large role in both my education and my involvement in gaelic football and hurling. Mr Paddy Woods taught me for the last six years in St Peter's Primary School. He was a brilliant teacher and I was not one bit surprised when he was recalled to teach in St Patrick's Teacher Training College. Mr Maurice (Mossy) O'Connor was also a great teacher, who gave a lifetime to the development of primary school sports. He was responsible for hundreds of young people playing gaelic sports and joining athletic clubs, including Paddy Holden and myself, who both went on to win All-Ireland senior football medals with Dublin.

Mr Ted Cooling is the third primary schoolteacher, who also gave a lifetime to the development of primary school sport. His car was always crammed with young players when we were playing an away game.

I have remained thankful to these three great men all of my life.

These three men also inspired me to eventually make education my career. I have had a wonderful and fulfilling experience working in education since returning home from the United States in the early 70s with a Masters in Sports Science. I am immensely grateful to my academic colleagues in Killester Vocational School, DIT Bolton St and DCU – it was a great honour to work alongside so many brilliant people. Equally, I always felt privileged to meet and help guide members of the student population in each of these places of learning.

FINALLY, TO MY teammates on the field of play, here in Ireland and in the U.S., can I offer a heartfelt thank you for so many amazing experiences. Both in victory and defeat it was my great pleasure to be by your side. And to those boys and girls, men and women, whom I have coached over the last half a century and more, thank you for giving me back every bit as much as I attempted to give you.

Mickey Whelan
January 2022

◀ ◁ ◆ ▷ ▶

IT HAS BEEN a privilege to work with Mickey over the past year and help to tell one of the great stories of Irish sport.

Despite our generation gap, Mickey was enthusiastic about working together from the get-go, and regaled his many memories with both passion and energy.

Whatever environment was permitted by the Covid-19 restrictions at a given moment, be it in DCU, over Zoom, or having a cup of tea in his back-garden, Mickey was always forthcoming in our many chats, and meticulous in his preparation. I hope he enjoyed telling his story as much as I did hearing it.

Thanks must also go to Mickey's family, as well as the many individuals who kindly shared their time to contribute their thoughts to this book. For other 'thoughts' on the life and times of Mickey Whelan, the following sources were much appreciated: *Jayo: My Autobiography* (Jason Sherlock), Mick Byrne (1995 interview with Liam Horan), Peter Brannigan (1995 interview with Liam Horan), Tommy Connolly (*Sunday Tribune*, 1997), Joe Hanrahan (*Sunday Tribune*, 1997),

Conal Keaney (*Sunday Independent*, 2021), and Jimmy Keaveny (*Irish Daily Mail*, 2011).

LIAM HAYES OF Hero Books could not have been more helpful, from initially broaching the possibility of working together on this book, to his guidance right throughout the entire process.

My editor in Sky Sports, Paul Prenderville was hugely supportive when I approached him about undertaking the project, facilitating it from day one.

Finally, to my parents Gerry and Noelle, thanks for the continued support and encouragement at every turn.

Brian Barry
January 2022

« PROLOGUE »

'We've been to hell and back over the last few years.

'I want to mention our management team. When they first took over, they had an unbelievable task on their hands… turning things around and getting us to where we are today. We've been fortunate enough to work with some unbelievable people… Pat Gilroy, David Hickey, Mickey Whelan, Paddy O'Donoghue… and everyone attached to this squad.

Unbelievable men who have not only lifted this [cup] as players, but join an elite group to have done it as players and management.

'On behalf of all the lads, I want to thank you from the bottom of my heart for the efforts you have put in.

'Thanks very much.'

ONCE BRYAN CULLEN finished his 2011 All-Ireland winning speech, it was pandemonium. Croke Park erupted.

Moments earlier, Stephen Cluxton had the composure and courage to score a late free to win the All-Ireland… Dublin's first in 16 years. Since the 70s, when a Dublin team inspired by Kevin Heffernan had put their stamp on the game by winning three All-Irelands in four glorious summers, there had only been two occasions when the Sam Maguire Cup had made itself at home in the capital city.

In 1983, when Heffo again watched over as 12 Dublin footballers famously defeated 14 Galwaymen, and in '95 when Pat O'Neill guided his team home against Tyrone.

Two All-Ireland titles.

Two decades.

Each victory gave Dublin supporters a taste of being the very best. Each time, the taste did not last for too long.

Would 2011 be any different? This time, there were solid foundations. This was no overnight success. Three years of blood, sweat and tears had gone into the act of Bryan Cullen climbing the steps of the Hogan Stand, and lifting Sam. In those three years, the Dublin manager Pat Gilroy, and his management team of Mickey Whelan, David Hickey and Paddy O'Donoghue, had searched the county far and wide for new talent.

There were 6am training sessions.

There were harsh lessons.

Tough defeats.

There were winters of reflection.

But Dublin were now back at the summit. More than that, the team's final strides to reach that exalted place had left Dublin's greatest and noblest opponent, beaten.

Kerry had been beaten!

It was a rare enough happening in the magnificent duel between gaelic football's two greatest exponents.

In truth, it was a blur after Stephen Cluxton hit the winning point into the Hill 16 end of Croke Park. But it was magical.

Mickey Whelan, like many ex-Dublin footballers, was overjoyed by the thrilling victory he had just witnessed, but that exquisite Sunday in 2011 was far too joyous to allow him any time to reflect on a time when he was a younger man out on that same field.

But, almost 50 years before, Mickey Whelan had been out there.

An All-Ireland title just captured.

A whole footballing life of brilliant promise still at his feet.

IN 1963, MICKEY Whelan kicked five points in the final against Galway to help Dublin win an All-Ireland. In 2011, he was sitting on the bench.

He watched as Stephen Cluxton took an age to walk up to the ball. When the Dublin goalkeeper eventually kicked it, the ground seemed to move. The stadium shook.

There was a tremor.

Mickey Whelan could hardly remember such noise in the home of the GAA. He never doubted Cluxton.

No. He had coached the team for the previous three years. He knew, and he expected. He had no doubt that, like everything else he did, Cluxton would be composed as he prepared to take his kick, and that he would be utterly clinical, before and after placing the ball.

The story goes that on his way up to the ball, Cluxton asked Rory O'Carroll to verify the amount of time remaining. It was 1-11 apiece in an All-Ireland final, against a team Dublin had only beaten twice in Mickey Whelan's lifetime.

And Mickey Whelan was born in 1939.

Seventy-one minutes had elapsed.

Two minutes of added time announced.

Mickey remained confident Stephen Cluxton was going to nail it.

But, he also knew that Cluxton was wily enough to make sure there would be no time for Kerry to work their way up and get an equaliser.

MINUTES EARLIER, KEVIN McManamon had stormed through for a goal.

McManamon had been unleashed late in the game. But all through the summer of 2011 he had been running the legs off tiring defenders late in games.

At the best of times, he would be hard to handle for any defender. Sixty minutes into an All-Ireland final, however, when a defender is growing weary, the last player he wanted to see running onto the field was McManamon.

A goal in the 64th minute of an All-Ireland final brought the gap down to one.

Mickey Whelan believed Dublin would win. Moments like that didn't just happen. *We're going to win this, no matter what transpires between now and the final whistle,* he told himself.

He believed that if Kerry were going to win the game, they were going to win it by three, four… five points.

That goal sucked the whole life out of Kerry. It lifted Dublin higher.

HE ALWAYS FANCIED Dublin if the All-Ireland final was going to go down the home straight. He knew the team's fitness would get them over the line. They weren't going to be found wanting for stamina.

'I'm not so sure other teams were doing the kind of work we were doing, over the course of those three years,' he explains. 'From the beginning there was always an element of speed, and speed endurance, involved in each training session. On occasions during training games, the game would be stopped and players would go to one side and spend 10 minutes doing five to six extra 20-metres sprints, with two minutes recovery between each sprint, and then return to continue the game at the original high tempo. They had fully bought into everything we asked them to do.

'At the start, in 2009, they might have wondered what was going on, but quickly enough every player bought into it. The end result was that we were always playing the final 10 minutes at the same pace as the opening 10.'

KERRY HAD LORDED it over Dublin for almost 80 years, barring a few years in the 70s when Mickey Whelan's closest friend, the *great* Kevin Heffernan, was in charge. Kerry were in Dublin heads for too long. That had to change.

In the first summer that Pat Gilroy was in charge, and Mickey Whelan took responsibility for the team's fitness, and skills and alertness, Kerry had hammered Dublin by 17 points in the 2009 All-Ireland quarter-final.

Six months after that humiliation, Dublin went down and beat Kerry in their own backyard in a National League game. It was a hugely important win. Dublin then backed it up in the following year's league.

The 2011 All-Ireland final win would help Dublin to become a superior force, over Kerry, and everyone else in the country, both physically and mentally.

Under Jim Gavin, who replaced Pat Gilory in 2013, Dublin would go on and win four more championship matches against Kerry.

Dublin got into Kerry heads. The table had turned.

◄ ◄◆▷ ►

PAT GILROY

Donegal were so strong and they were doing so much damage to teams… I had an eye on them and how I wanted us to play [in the final] and I didn't spend enough time on

Mayo. I would blame myself very strongly for allowing them to get that 10-point lead, because I hadn't put the same focus in. It's one thing I certainly would pin on myself.

It's where Mickey would have been excellent. He would have been probing and asking more about them. I had spent a little bit too much time looking at Donegal… looking at them as the real danger that year.

◄ ◄ ◆ ► ►

PAT GILROY HAD kindly acknowledged that Mickey's absence was telling in 2012, when Dublin fell to Mayo at the All-Ireland semi-final stage.

Maybe he was right, or maybe he was being kind to his old friend.

Mickey could only wonder.

The 2011 All-Ireland final was his last match with that group of Dublin footballers. Gilroy, and Paddy O'Donoghue and David Hickey, stayed on for the following year.

MICKEY FIRST MET Irene McGrath when he was 18 and she was 17 years old. He knew straight away she was the woman he wanted to marry, the woman with whom he wanted to spend the rest of his life with.

But, to begin with, he didn't think he was worthy of her. 'She was my rock. She was the best thing that ever happened to me.

'We married in 1965. She raised our five children. Each of them is a credit to their mother. When I moved to America in 1969, she followed me out. She was delayed getting over due to visa issues, so I was on my own out there for six months. That was the only Christmas we ever spent apart.

'In 2011, Irene was diagnosed with a blood problem.

'I knew from that moment that I would be leaving the Dublin management team at the end of the season. After the All-Ireland win, I said to her, "Irene, I'd like to step down now".

'She reminded me that I loved what I was doing with Dublin.

'I told her I was finished. "You know yourself… it's better to bow out now when we're winning".

'She asked me was I sure? I told her I was.

'And we spent two more years together.'

« CHAPTER 1 »

IN 2008, MICKEY Whelan was asked to join Pat Gilroy's management ticket for the Dublin senior football team. Externally, Gilroy was viewed as a surprise choice for the top job.

Months earlier, Gilroy and Whelan had won the All-Ireland Club Championship together... but as manager and player. Gilroy was a key member in that St Vincent's side, but Whelan had to twist his arm to give it one more year at the start of the 2007 season.

Now, the Vincent's No 14 wanted the Vincent's team manager on the Dublin sideline with him.

Mickey had no doubts that Pat Gilroy was destined to be a successful manager himself.

'Pat is a bright guy, and is successful in a professional environment. He knows how to manage people,' says Mickey, '... through business as well as football! He had also built up a great deal of experience on the field, winning an All-Ireland in 1995.'

Whelan had played with Pat's late father Jackie Gilroy; a staunch Vinnies' man, who was unlucky to miss out on an All-Ireland in 1963. Jackie had died too young, in 2007.

He knew Pat would be able to measure up to the massive task at hand in attempting to lead Dublin to an All-Ireland title. But he was also aware of a great deal of chatter at the time of the announcement.

'Pat and I were compared in the media to Steve Staunton and Bobby Robson (a pairing that had taken over the Irish soccer team two years previously). We were likened to the pair, whose time in charge didn't work out the way they would have wanted,' remembers Mickey.

'People were saying that an old mentor and a young manager will never work out. But when you take a job like that, you need to block out the noise.'

THIRTEEN YEARS EARLIER, Mickey Whelan had taken the Dublin management job himself.

Pat O'Neill had just led Dublin to their first All-Ireland title in 12 years, before vacating the post. It was a busy time for Whelan on the coaching front. He was working with Dundalk FC, helping them to the League of Ireland title alongside Dermot Keely when he was initially appointed.

He was lecturing in Dublin Institute of Technology, and had managed DIT to two national gaelic football titles around the time. He was also working with the Dublin hurlers.

After being interviewed, he was given the Dublin job.

'Was it a great ambition of mine to manage Dublin one day?' he asks. 'No. I had helped Kevin Heffernan from afar in the 70s when he was in the top job, but as regards to personal ambition to be the centre of attention? Not at all.

'I brought Lorcan Redmond and Christy Kane in as selectors. They had experience, which is crucial. Lorcan had worked alongside Kevin with Dublin. And he is a good guy. I needed somebody that I knew well. I had worked with him myself.

'I had played with Christy. He was another member of the team that won an All-Ireland in 1963, and I also lined out alongside him with Clanna Gael.'

AFTER YEARS OF coming close, Dublin had finally gotten over the line in 1995, beating Tyrone 1-10 to 0-12 in the All-Ireland final. They had been through a lot in the previous decade – including a four-game saga with Meath a few years previously. No matter what they tried to do over that famous month in June of 1991, they were unable to put the Royals away.

They also lost two All-Ireland finals in that troublesome period of time, before edging Tyrone.

The 1995 victory did require a steely determination, and some luck. Tyrone's talisman Peter Canavan was blown up for fisting the ball along the ground in the run-up to a score. But it was legal at that time to knock the ball away from you when you were on the ground. Dublin prevailed by a point.

In 1996, under Mickey Whelan's watch, Dublin would lose their Leinster and All-Ireland titles, when they were surprised by a young Meath team in the provincial final.

In 1997, Dublin did not make it to the Leinster final.

LOOKING BACK, WOULD Mickey Whelan have done anything different in his two years in charge?

He says absolutely not.

'I went back into the Dublin squad 13 years later, in 2009. They hadn't won another All-Ireland since 1995. I didn't do anything different between 2009 and '11 than I had done in 1996 and '97.'

When he was appointed in 1996, he believed that some change was needed to refreshen a squad that had been on the road in search of an elusive All-Ireland for so long. He called up Ciaran Whelan, Paddy Christie and Ian Robertson during that timeframe.

Joe McNally had fallen away from the squad in 1992, and missed out on a Celtic Cross in '95. Many thought he was finished. But Whelan saw one of the best club players in the county, hands-down, and he decided to bring him back into the team. He also brought Eamonn Heery back in; he was playing well. Niall Guiden too. He made Keith Barr captain, in order to get more out of him. He was centre-back, and playing really well. Barr replaced John O'Leary in the captaincy role.

MICKEY WHELAN'S TWO years on the Dublin sideline would prove disappointing, and bruising. But, amongst other things, Mickey was a fighter.

Literally, as a much younger man, he *was* a fighter.

He wasn't one to walk away.

But, after two years, and in the face of some dissatisfaction from players, and some abuse from disgruntled supporters, he took the decision to leave the job.

He took the decision calmly, and clinically.

'Growing up in Cabra West, I had boxed in the tech school, though I rarely had to call on those skills on the field of play. But I had them in the locker…

'I say *rarely*, rather than *never*, because I did have to pull them out in the 1963 All-Ireland final. The Galway centre-back Seán Meade was at me, and I hit him. He was likely looking to antagonise me.

'My father and his twin brother Matt had boxed in the army. After that 1963 final, I remember coming home to shower before going out to the function. There was a crowd in our house celebrating. Matt pulled me aside to congratulate me.

'He told me… "I liked that one-two!"

'I was always able to stand up for myself when the occasion demanded it.'

◄ ◄ ◆ ► ►

JASON SHERLOCK

What I can say with absolute certainty with the benefit of hindsight is that Mickey was the right man at the wrong time.

When he eventually stepped away from the job, he reckoned we didn't buy into his system and he is probably right. But he was 20 years ahead of his time and it's hardly surprising that the lads didn't see the bigger picture.

The innovative ideas he had gleaned abroad ran counter to the GAA philosophy of coaching, which maintained you hadn't really trained hard unless you ended up bent over and puking. Mickey was big into sports science long before the GAA was ready for it.

The squad was now skipping to an altogether new rhythm. No more of the never-ending, mind-numbing cross-country… we became 'less is more' advocates. All of Mickey's training was based around the football. He wasn't developing athletes, but unfortunately that was an approach that had never sat well with inter-county teams of old.

It's called games-based training these days, but back then we wanted all the flogging an inter-county player was supposed to get. It was never a slog and that seemed unusual. Mickey would bellow, 'Money in the bank, fellas,' although some lads were questioning whether we were putting enough cash away to prepare us for the intense battles ahead during the Leinster Championship.

Mickey's ideas about strength and conditioning are now the norm and it's obvious he was a pioneer. But back in 1996 the Dublin team was an ageing unit and some of the senior players were probably too set in their ways to depart from a tried-and-trusted route mapped and paved through years of persistence

◄ ◄ ◆ ▷ ►

THE FIRST BOX Mickey Whelan wanted to tick when he took the Dublin reins in 1996 – and it is the first thing he did with any team he ever coached – was to get them fit. Get them fit… with the ball.

Not just running drills. He incorporated the ball into proceedings.

He would do sprinting drills. But he'd do sprinting drills, and use the ball. Players were sprinting, getting the ball, giving it off… then sprinting 30 yards.

'Nobody stops. One player is sprinting, taking the ball on the left, giving it to someone on the right… taking another ball on the right… going left. All in that 30-metre area… always sprinting.

'If they let the ball fall, nobody stops. They keep going.

'I am getting them to feed and collect the ball under stress, and they have to be good passers as well. There is no standing, no getting cold. It is all ball-work… soloing, sprinting, shooting… or kick-passing at the end.

'Then we go into small-sided games, concentrating on tackling with the ball… one-on-one, two-on-two. Making it a physical contest, getting used to a war of attrition.

'The beauty of working with the ball is that you're getting the players fit without it being labelled as *fitness training* in their minds.'

IT STARTED WELL with the Dublin squad. They were flying in 1996, playing some really good football. The first championship match was a Leinster quarter-final against Westmeath in Navan.

Barney Rock had taken charge of Westmeath, and they were being talked up in the media. Dublin were supposed to be walking into a trap. But Dublin played brilliantly, winning 1-18 to 0-11. They had 11 different scorers, with McNally kicking 0-3 and Barr scoring the goal.

After the match, one of the Dublin players admitted, 'It felt like I could run all day, but we don't really seem to be doing a huge amount of fitness work. Whatever he's doing, we don't feel like it's really hard stuff. But I can't believe how fit I am'.

Next up in the semi-final was Louth, a team Whelan had managed nine years beforehand.

McNally was crucial again, this time scoring a goal. That helped Dublin to a 1-9 to 0-8 win, and they were back into the Leinster final. Against Meath.

Dublin were coming into the provincial decider in a good place. They were playing well, and had built up momentum. On balance, that Leinster final might have been the best game Dublin played in those two years.

'We played well, and led by two points after 59 minutes,' Mickey remembers.

'They took the lead, but we had a goal disallowed in injury-time. They won 0-10 to 0-8. Meath went on and won the All-Ireland title.

'Gaelic football is a game of narrow margins.

'That showed itself again in 1997. We drew Meath in the Leinster Championship opener. They were reigning champions, but we fancied our chances.

'They beat us 1-13 to 1-10. Paul Bealin rattled the bar from a late penalty.

'Fine margins indeed.'

◄◄◆►►

SEÁN BOYLAN

When you look back at those games with crossbars being hit... things like that, it must have been very frustrating for Mickey.

There was never much between us. In 1995, we led Dublin in the second-half but lost by 10 points. They won the All-Ireland. They ended up on the wrong side the following year.

But he was never interested in the blame game. It was always a case of, 'What can we do from here?' I have been watching Mickey Whelan my whole life, and his philosophy has always been... 'How can we improve? How can we make things better from here?'

Now human nature being what it is – we're amateurs and we celebrate and that's a fact – the Dublin players were coming down off the highs of 1995.

Maybe for a lot of the Dublin players, 1995 was somewhat of a swansong. They had endured hard years and near misses in 1994, '93 and '92, as well as our famous matches in '91.

We caught them on the hop in 1996.

Mickey Whelan's teams were very smart. Nobody emphasised the simplicity of the game better than him.

He brought a great science to it. Even when it came to people with stats, Mickey would get disturbed by people coming up to tell him how many times something happened in a match. In the computer of Mickey's mind, they were telling him something that he already knew!

Even in his warm-ups, in his preparations, instead of people expending all the energy in the warm-up, per say, he had a great knack of getting people to conserve energy. In competition, the whole secret is being able to take that pressure, physically and mentally and get on with the job.

I remember in one of those matches against us, he would be down on the sideline near Hill 16 on the Cusack Stand side. If someone hesitated, he was on-hand to deliver a message... 'Take your chances when you get them'.

He'd almost remind you of a hunter, or someone stranded on an island. He taught people how to hunt, in the same way he always encouraged players to do the right thing. He did that endlessly, time after time with any team he coached.

I'd say if he was there as Dublin manager for longer in the 90s, it would have been a different story.

◄◄◆▷►

THERE ARE A few myths around Mickey Whelan's two years in the mid-90s as Dublin team boss.

It was reported that he brought Kevin Heffernan into the set-up. His great friend had travelled on the team bus to an away match, sparking rumours.

However, Heffo's presence on the bus was far more simple than that!

At that stage, Kevin Heffernan couldn't drive, and Lorcan Redmond had told him that he could travel with the team, if he wanted to go away to the match in question. It was nothing more than an act of friendship between a group of very old and loyal friends.

But Heffo's presence grew legs. *Unhelpful legs.*

Then, in what proved to be Whelan's penultimate match in charge of Dublin, the team was playing away to Sligo in a league game.

As he often did throughout his coaching career, Whelan entrusted the captain to oversee the warm-up. He liked to give power and responsibility to his players. But this time, this decision was picked up completely in the wrong context. Journalists construed that, 'Mickey Whelan had lost the dressing-room' and that Keith Barr had taken charge of the warm-up. It was completely untrue.

'That was my way of doing things,' Mickey explains. 'I wanted the players to take the lead, be part of it… assume leadership.

'The reports were taken up the wrong way, and they fuelled the push against me. Indeed, they inspired some of the ill-will that was evident two weeks later in Parnell Park.'

ULTIMATELY, MICKEY WHELAN walked away with no regrets about the job he did. In the following years, however, he had a heavy heart as he watched Offaly, Kildare, Meath, Laois and Westmeath all win Leinster Championships… as Dublin struggled.

'We didn't win the Sam Maguire in my period as manager, but I'm not sure anybody could have done any more for the team during that time.

'I didn't change my approach. I went away, and worked elsewhere implementing the same philosophies. I helped to win titles with DIT and Dundalk FC around that time, once I had full buy-in from players.'

◄ ◄ ◆ ► ►

JASON SHERLOCK

Mickey was hurt at the time but history would ultimately be kind to him. As a trainer he was less hills and drills and more about skills.

He won an All-Ireland club title with St Vincent's in 2008 and played a vital role in Dublin's 2011 senior title as coach alongside Pat Gilory. The reputation that took such a battering between 1995 and '97 was thoroughly restored over time. He was, in fact, one of the good guys. One of the great football men. It just took people a long time to get that.

PAT GILROY

The thing was on its way down by the time Mickey took charge, and that was the reality of it. It probably took that team too long to get to the top. And we probably had put in so much in the previous four or five years that it was a team that probably won an All-Ireland on the way down the hill, rather than on the way up the hill.

Young players had to be introduced, and there were hard decisions that needed to be made. It was a tough time to take on a team that had just won an All-Ireland.

I was one of the younger ones, and I had been there for four or five years. We had trained extremely hard. I think everybody was tired having got there eventually after so many failures. We really probably should have won it earlier, but we didn't.

Mickey introduced a very different style of training, maybe to suit the older guys as well. They weren't going to be able to be flogged again, because they didn't have it in the legs. I think some of them felt that they needed to do the same thing as the year before. The truth was… if we had done the same thing, we wouldn't even have got past the first round.

It was just one of those things.

Things happen to you in life, and you just have to move on from them.

IT ALL ENDED on a November Sunday in Parnell Park in 1997. Dublin were playing Offaly in a National League game. By that stage, some of the criticism had become unacceptable to Mickey Whelan.

'I was well able for the flack. But it was unfair on Irene… and unfair on my children. It all came to the boil when Offaly came to Donnycarney.

'Tommy Lyons' side beat us, and there was a poisonous atmosphere.

'At full-time, a young girl ran over and told me I was a disgrace. Now a 12-year-old girl did not necessarily arrive at that mindset by herself. It was likely a regurgitation of what she had heard from a parent. Maybe it was innocuous, but for me it was the straw that broke the camel's back.

'I didn't need that. I walked into the dressing-room.

'I told the players I was leaving. I walked upstairs and informed John Costello.

'He asked me not to step down.

'I told him I had made up my mind.

'I walked out, and past a group of assembled journalists, all waiting to get a line as rumours circled around Parnell Park. There were a flurry of questions.

'I didn't stop.'

It was a great honour for Mickey Whelan to coach Dublin to a breakthrough All-Ireland victory over Kerry in 2011 and to celebrate the homecoming (above) with an amazing group of footballers. But, in fact, he did nothing different in working with the players than he did when he was manager of Dublin (below) 15 years earlier.

« CHAPTER 2 »

PAT GILROY'S APPOINTMENT as Dublin manager in late-2008 was indeed met with surprise in some quarters.

Gilroy was not long retired from playing, having won a club All-Ireland just months beforehand.

For Gilroy, that St Patrick's Day triumph was his swansong. A last hurrah.

He was not planning for it to be that way, however. Mickey Whelan had to convince him to give it one more go before the 2007 season began. Gilroy was quickly becoming successful in his professional life. Mickey told him, 'You're going to be a busy man. You've got to keep yourself fit'.

And he quoted Kevin Heffernan… 'Nobody retires in Vincent's… you just fade away. You should keep training with us.

'You should come up. It would be good for yourself, good for the younger guys on the squad… and good for your kids.'

After a few weeks, the league got underway. Whelan mentioned to Gilroy that he should consider togging out for another season.

'Jesus Mickey… I've five kids!'

'Well talk to your wife!' came the reply.

On teams Whelan managed, he always ensured players' partners were well looked after. He believed they were the ones making all the sacrifices, not the players. Players were in it for the glory of winning. Their partners were the ones putting up with it, when the players were missing a few nights a week because of training, or having a quiet weekend while resting for a match. 'Have a chat with her, Pat.' Off home Pat Gilroy went.

He was on the phone to Whelan very quickly. He agreed to play another year.

Kevin Heffernan always said that St Vincent's men don't retire. He ingrained that in Mickey and others.

It was a message passed onto Pat Gilroy. Gilroy played for one final year in 2007, which stretched into '08. *And did he enjoy a memorable final chapter!*

FOR MICKEY WHELAN, that 2008 All-Ireland club victory was in many ways some redemption on the national landscape.

To do it with the club, however, was extra special.

Even though St Vincent's was not always Whelan's club.

He would become club president, long after winning the All-Ireland Club Championship as both a player and a manager. In 1981, he managed the footballers and trained the hurlers as Vincent's won the Dublin Senior Championship double in the club's 50th jubilee year.

But, Mickey was once a whole different clubman.

GROWING UP, HE always played with Clanna Gael. Though born in Cabra West, he went out to Ringsend, as one of his primary schoolteachers in Phibsboro, Mossy O'Connor pointed a few young lads in that direction.

Mickey had great times over the years there, peaking in 1968 when the club won the Dublin Senior Championship, when he was a player-manager.

In 1969, he was named captain of the Dublin senior footballers, as Kevin Heffernan was taking charge, ahead of what would prove to be a remarkable spell of success for the Dublin football team.

That was on a Wednesday.

That Saturday, Kevin was driving his friend out to Dublin airport.

Mickey Whelan was emigrating to the United States.

Six years later, in the mid-70s, after the family's return from the U.S., Whelan never imagined he would become a St Vincent's man.

The family moved back into the house in Sutton Park that he and Irene had bought the previous decade.

'While Clanna Gael was not exactly the local club for me in Sutton Park, getting to Ringsend was nonetheless doable. But when I returned after six years of travels and studies, the club where I had played for so many years had upped sticks. They were now elsewhere on the southside,' Mickey explains.

'In truth, it was too big an ask to cross the city to the other side of the county. Not only because of the time involved, but also the cost of petrol. I was starting back on the lowest rung of the teaching ladder. It would have been too expensive.

'At this stage, I was in my late-thirties, and had a young family. Perhaps it was time to hang up the boots. I went looking for Ted Coolin, the president of Clanna Gael. He was living in Raheny, and had just had an accident with his eye, so wasn't allowed to drive. He had a friend who was a member of Vincent's, and had roped him into a bit of coaching there.

'Ted said to me, "I'm there… why don't you bring your kids down to Vincent's?"

'Not long afterwards, I found myself in Marino… coaching underage.'

OF COURSE, MICKEY was not back on the old sod for long before Kevin Heffernan had him training teams. He asked Mickey to do a bit of coaching with the Vinnies' intermediate footballers.

'I found myself coaching the club's second team, as Kevin was busy guiding the senior team to the 1975 Dublin Championship.

'After a training session one evening, Brendan Pocock, and the president of the club Emmet Memery, knocked around to my house.

'They wanted to come in and have a chat.

'I thought I had done something wrong!

'They sat me down, and told me they wanted me to play for the intermediate footballers.

' "But I can't," I told them… "I'm a *Clanna Gael man!*"

'Emmet told me I was a… *Vincent's man!*'

After some thinking, Whelan was beginning to come around to the idea. But first he needed to get Ted Coolin's blessing.

He needed Ted's permission.

'Himself and Mossy O'Connor. I felt really loyal to them, and they were very loyal to me. They understood what the situation was, once I explained it to them.

'I got the green light to pull on the white and blue jersey of Vincent's.'

HE HADN'T PLAYED with Clanna Gael in over six years, but he was still actively playing over on the other side of the Atlantic Ocean.

Mickey had also been playing soccer at a high level. He was fit, and he was certainly going to be able to do a job for the Vincent's second team.

So he agreed to tog out.

One of the first games was an intermediate final against northside rivals Na Fianna. He had been coaching the team, but now Mickey was lacing up his boots. It was around a time that St Vincent's were declared county senior champions – the Dublin County Board awarded them the title after UCD refused to fulfil the final fixture. They were preparing for the first round of the Leinster Club Championship, the day after the Dublin intermediate decider.

Na Fianna beat Vincent's by a point.

'Moments after full-time, I was standing on the pitch. And I remember this like it was yesterday. My nostrils suddenly filled with a familiar scent of tobacco that could only be one man. I heard a voice over my shoulder.

' "If you had any help there, you'd have won that match by yourself!"

'I turned around.

'Kevin Heffernan had appeared from virtually nowhere. Before I could muster a response, his next statement was… "I'm not starting you tomorrow down in Slane, but I'm bringing you on at half time.

'He turned and began walking away from me. I told him to hold on a second. "What are you talking about? I'm retired! I'm not playing".

'He told me he didn't bring me to Vincent's to play intermediate football.

'That was that. What Kevin said was gospel!

'But lining out for the Vincent's seniors was a big problem for me. Getting my arm twisted to play an intermediate match was one thing. *How would the Clanna Gael lads look at this one?* I was now going to play senior football.

'And how would the St Vincent's players take me?

'I was going to be taking somebody's place on the team, or if I was a substitute I would be knocking someone else down the pecking order.

'It didn't look like I had a choice, however. Kevin was one of my closest friends. We were inseparable. So, the next day, along I went. I was really embarrassed going down to this one, because I knew there were guys going to be left off.

'Kevin put me on in the second-half. We got over the line, and won the game.'

WITHOUT PLAYING A second of action in the Dublin Championship that year, Mickey Whelan was now on a team that was gaining momentum in the province and eyeing up an All-Ireland title.

He was lining out beside some of the biggest names in gaelic football at the time... Jimmy Keaveny, Brian Mullins and Tony Hanahoe. St Vincent's came through Leinster, beating Tinryland of Carlow and St Joseph's of Laois. St Vincent's were then faced with a tricky All-Ireland semi-final draw.

Nemo Rangers... in Cork.

It was very much a revenge mission for the rest of the Vincent's team, after Nemo had beaten them in an All-Ireland final replay three years beforehand.

Nemo were favourites, but everything clicked for the Dublin team that day. It was a heavy pitch at the Mardyke. Keaveny kicked six points from frees, as they ran out 0-10 to 0-3 winners. It could have been a lot more.

The Dublin representatives have been training at full stretch under Kevin Heffernan for the past 10 weeks, and the hand of the maestro was clearly evident, wrote *Irish Times* journalist, Paddy Downey in a match report entitled... *ST VINCENT'S WORTH MUCH BIGGER VICTORY.*

They played textbook football. They were masters in the air. In most positions two or three men almost invariably converged on a single opponent when a ball was being contested; their teamwork and running were a replica of the style of the Dublin county team and to these attributes were added the inestimable bonus of endless energy and superior speed.

And so, St Vincent's were through to the All-Ireland final against Roscommon Gaels, with the match set for Portlaoise. The job was far from complete.

'We weren't taking anything for granted, and that's why we hammered them.

'Kevin Heffernan wouldn't have allowed any complacency to seep in. We went out there, expecting to have a great team playing against us. They were fresh from winning a second consecutive Connacht Championship, and were coming for the big one. We saw them as the best team we were going to play. It was as simple as that. In the end, we annihilated them.

'4-10 to 0-5 was the final score.'

On a miserable wet day, the contest was decided as early as 10 minutes into the first-half. St Vincent's were facing an extremely strong wind in this period, and when they were leading by a goal and a point after only eight minutes, it was obvious that the title would go to them, read one match report.

Jimmy Keaveney opened the scoring in the third minute with a pointed free and then, in the eighth minute the veteran Mickey Whelan scored a decisive goal when he crashed the ball to the net off an upright.

◄ ◄ ◆ ► ►

BRIAN MULLINS

In 1975 when Mickey returned from America, he didn't initially play senior football. He played a lower grade with the club. There were a number of months where he wasn't part of the senior team, until we were playing in the Leinster Club Championship.

He started lining out for the club.

We all originally thought he would be staying with that team. We didn't realise he would graduate to the senior level. I don't think his own plan was to play senior football either, but obviously Kevin Heffernan, who would have been instrumental in him joining the club, had different ideas. The fact he had been in America for the past six years meant that the Clanna Gael involvement was hugely diminished, if that's the right word.

We won the All-Ireland club in April 1976. Uniquely, we were successful in that competition but we didn't qualify through the traditional route of winning the Dublin Championship.

Mickey's arrival into the mix was part coincidental, part designed by Kevin Heffernan. We didn't expect, up to a certain point, that we would be taking part in the Leinster Championship and All-Ireland series, because in offering us the opportunity, the Dublin County Board also offered to award us the county championship.

We refused to accept that.

Even though we represented Dublin in Leinster and subsequently the All-Ireland series, we weren't champions in any way of Dublin.

A lot of us were surprised that Mickey was able to perform so well at senior level. He had spent six years in America, and was in his late-thirties at this stage.

He was coming from an environment where he had played mostly soccer in America. But once he got back into playing initially before moving onto senior football, the old instincts and his natural ability came to the fore very quickly.

We were beaten in 1973 by Nemo Rangers after a replay. When we met again three years later, we won by seven points. In the interim, a number of our team had garnered huge experience on the inter-county scene, winning the All-Ireland in 1974.

Bobby Doyle, Tony Hanahoe, Gay O'Driscoll, Jimmy Keaveney and myself... we were all brought on by playing at that high level.

But Mickey's arrival also added value and was a factor.

He made a significant difference.

◄ ◄ ◆ ▷ ►

IN MARCH 1976, the All-Ireland Club Championship was in its relative infancy. There was no St Patrick's Day slot for the decider. There was no Croke Park stage.

At full-time in Portlaoise on a rainy day, the man that presented the cup walked out with it under his coat, handed it to Jimmy Keaveney and said, 'There you go boys!' And that was it. No speech. No nothing!

But as far as St Vincent's and Kevin Heffernan were concerned, that didn't matter. The win was everything.

That year was only the competition's sixth iteration.

There was no such thing as a Leinster Club Championship when Clanna Gael won the county title eight years previously.

◄ ◄ ◆ ▷ ►

THE VINCENT'S TEAM that won that All-Ireland Club Championship in March 1976 provided the backbone for the Dublin team that was in the midst of a run of three Sam Maguire Cup triumphs in four years.

Kevin Heffernan, of course, was the man behind those successes. After the win over Roscommon Gaels, his focus immediately turned fully back to the county set-up.

Around that same time, Mickey Whelan went over to his house one day.

Kevin hit him with the proposition... 'Would you not come back in with Dublin?'

At this stage, Whelan was almost 37. He had a young family, and was working his way up in the teaching world, having completed his studies.

Kevin Heffernan always found a way to twist Mickey's arm, right up until his passing in 2013. Heffo was a brilliant man for bringing everyone around to his way of thinking! But Mickey had to draw the line.

He was not going to return to the inter-county scene.

Heffo being *Heffo*, he wasn't going to give up without a fight, and was exploring different avenues.

Mary Heffernan, Kevin's wife, was standing on a counter in the house, painting the wall behind it. She came to Mickey's rescue!

'He said no, Kevin… leave him alone. Mickey, don't listen to him!' Eventually, Heffo got the message.

Mickey had Mary to thank for getting him out of that one!

◄◄◆►►

MICKEY WON AN All-Ireland medal with St Vincent's without winning a county medal with the club. But it wasn't long until that was corrected.

The 70s were a golden period for Dublin football. And the decade wasn't working out too badly for St Vincent's either.

In 1976 and '77, he collected his second and third Dublin SFC medals, as Vincent's beat UCD and Synge Street Past Pupils (now Templeogue Synge Street) in the two finals.

Though now in his very late-thirties, he was by no means a peripheral player.

Eventually, the time came to hang up the boots.

'I had left it all on the field. It was time to step aside. Not that I was walking away from football altogether. In fact, I remained involved as ever, but on the sideline. Many who go into coaching after their own career ends say that they can never replicate the buzz of playing.

'For me, I had been coaching for over a decade. I had won a Dublin SFC title as a player-manager with Clanna Gael in 1968. I was coaching throughout my years in the United States.

'I was even helping Kevin Heffernan coach the Dublin team from afar. When I returned to Ireland, I remained coaching.

'For me, it was a natural transition to the sideline.

'For many, finishing their playing career is the end.

'For me, I was only getting started.'

Kevin Heffernan (top) played a huge role in
Mickey's life and he was lucky to be able to
call him a friend, teammate and colleague.

When he returned from the U.S.
in the mid-70s Mickey also got to
reunite with old Dublin teammates
Jimmy Keaveney and Tony Hanahoe
(above right) when he joined St
Vincent's. He also got to play with
the brilliant Brian Mullins.

« CHAPTER 3 »

HALF THE DUBLIN squad might have thought Mickey Whelan was crazy when he began dragging them out of their beds for 6am training sessions in 2009 and the years that followed.

He wanted to toughen them up mentally. Too often the team had come through Leinster, winning the province with ease. But when it came to the cut and thrust of knockout football in the All-Ireland series, Dublin were coming up short.

Other teams could handle the pressure. Dublin were beating the likes of Meath and Wexford in Leinster, but *the likes* of Meath and Wexford were the ones reaching All-Ireland semi-finals!

Part of the plan to toughen them up was to assemble for early morning training sessions. *Very early morning... 6am.*

It was also to toughen them up physically.

The other bonus was that Pat Gilroy and Whelan could get huge amounts of work done in just two days. They trained early in the morning, getting the hard work done. And they then assembled in the evening after everyone was finished work, for ball-work and a match.

They did that on Tuesdays and Thursdays, with four training sessions sandwiched into two days. Add in a match or training at the weekend, and that meant players only had to commit three days a week to the cause, rather than spreading the five sessions across five days.

After initial doubts, the feedback was massively positive. Even their employers were delighted – the players were up and about early in the morning, and were arriving at work alert and sprightly! Rather than rolling out of bed at the last minute, and landing into work with a slice of toast in hand.

'WE DID THE hard slog on the field, and then had breakfast together. That helped them bond as a group.

'The other aspect was, we were capitalising on one of Dublin's natural advantages. Not every county could do such early morning training, because their players needed to make longer commutes.

'We were at the bottom of the mountain, but as we put in the hard yards on those dark, winter mornings, we knew for a fact that Kerry and Tyrone were still in their beds.

'I'd say people thought it was mad. *It was mad,* I suppose.

'But it was mad in the right way. The thing was, it had already worked when I was manager of Vincent's. And the few lads from the club on the Dublin squad knew it. It wasn't long before the rest of the panel came to realise just how valuable an exercise it really was.'

◄◄◆►►

ALAN BROGAN

In the initial chats we had as a group, Pat Gilroy and Mickey laid it on the table that we'd failed up to now.

Once we laid the cards on the table and the group took on a very honest approach, lads at that stage were willing to do whatever it would take.

Obviously it was difficult getting up in the morning. But if Pat and Mickey and the management team were willing to show that commitment, then it was easy for us to follow that. It wasn't the fact that we were training at 6am… it was the levels of commitment guys were willing to show at that stage… turning up before they went to work. They wanted to see who was really committed to it, who could hack that level of intensity. We were training on Tuesday and Thursday mornings and Tuesday and

Thursday evenings for a period of time. Mickey's thinking was probably the scientific approach that if you train twice in the one day, you then get a full day's rest.

I don't think it was much to do with the physical thing at all. I think it was more the mental side of it that Mickey wanted to see playing its part... see who could stand up to it.

When you're in the melting pot at Croke Park in late August or September, they're the questions that are going to be asked. And Pat and Mickey probably would have weeded out a couple of guys who they felt... 'These guys probably aren't up to it when the pressure comes on'.

At the training sessions, he wasn't afraid to let lads have it if needed, in a respectful manner. You knew when Mickey shouted, you knew he was doing it for the betterment of the team, and the betterment of yourself. And guys really responded to that.

There were sessions where Mickey just wanted to bring us to the well and make us suffer as much as we possibly could. He wanted to push us as far as we could go, in order to build us up mentally.

But for the most part, everything was thought through. He was very strong on rest periods, which obviously became very important. He was very strong on nutrition. He had a lot of experience from his time in America.

At stages, Pat and Mickey in a weird sort of way took a bit of enjoyment out of putting guys through that sort of punishment. Mickey has lived and breathed coaching for so long. There was nothing more important than this to him, and nothing more important than getting that Dublin team ready to play in Croke Park.

And Pat would have been the same. And the rest of the management had that mentality. That mirrored itself onto the way the team prepared itself.

◄ ◄ ◆ ► ►

WHEN MICKEY WAS manager of the St Vincent's senior footballers in 2006, they lost the county final to UCD, 0-10 to 0-9. It was a defeat that was hard to swallow.

Dave Billings – a Vincent's man – had assembled an All Star team in Belfield, with Malachy O'Rourke as manager. It was an inter-county team, rather than a club side. Players from all over the country were coming in and playing a starring role, despite the fact they also played in their home club championships.

Offaly's Niall McNamee got them over the line in that final in Parnell Park. The win meant he was then in the Leinster Championship with two clubs, after Rhode won their county title!

'Offaly's Niall McNamee… Mayo's Austin O'Malley… Louth's Shane Lennon… Fermanagh's James Sherry… it was an inter-county team!' says Mickey.

In that final, there were suggestions that UCD had fielded an ineligible player. Some St Vincent's players weren't happy. Mickey wasn't happy to have lost the game. Vincent's hadn't won a Dublin senior title in 22 years, and now they had been beaten in dubious circumstances.

'There's a philosophy in Vincent's – if you're beaten on the field, you're beaten on the field. You don't appeal. You don't complain,' Mickey emphasises.

'We still should have won it. We didn't play our best football, despite having ample possession. But we didn't take the opportunities.

'After that loss, I decided to walk away, and let somebody else take charge. I was shattered by that defeat, and disillusioned.

'That was the plan, anyway.'

'A FEW WEEKS later, I came home one evening. Irene said to me, "Well, we're off, Michael. Your dinner is there!"

'The first I had heard about it… where are you all going?' I asked.

Irene was off to a concert in the Point Depot with her daughters.

Normally, she would always invite Mickey too. He would go sometimes, and other times he wouldn't. But there was no invite forthcoming that night. His wife just said… 'We're off'.

'What about me?' I joked.

'She said it was a girls' night out… "We're off!"

'And that was that. I was left to my own devices for the evening. I was just finished up eating… when I heard a knock on the door.

'Out I went, and who was standing just outside the porch lighting up a cigarette, but Kevin Heffernan.

'I knew exactly why he was there, before he even opened his mouth.'

Before Heffo said a thing, Mickey told him he was not going back!

'You can forget about it. It's done!'

Heffo just smiled.

'Are you going to let me in?' he asked. 'I just want to have a chat with you!'

Mickey stepped back from the door.

'Okay… but I'm not going back!'

Heffo stepped inside and said, 'We'll talk about it!' He didn't seem to be taking no for an answer.

He sat down at the kitchen table, and worked his way through a few cigarettes. Kevin Heffernan was the only person who ever smoked in the Whelan house. Irene didn't smoke, and neither did Mickey.

Heffo was lighting a cigarette as he walked in.

With Kevin working his way through the pack, the two men began to shoot the breeze. They were chatting about all sorts of subjects, but Heffo kept returning to the possibility of Mickey returning for another year in charge of Vincent's.

Each time, Mickey shot him down.

He kept coming at it another way and another way, and Mickey would say, 'No, it's over. That's it'. And then he'd go again… another cigarette. The pile on the makeshift ashtray – a saucer – was steadily growing. Mickey estimates there must have been 20 of them smoked that night.

They spent almost two and a half hours chatting. It was getting late. Then Kevin Heffernan said, 'Listen, you know… just do this for me, once… one more time, for me.

'Just one last time. Just for me…

'One more time and we'll let you free next year,' he said. 'We can't let this go. You're the only person who can do this. You have to do it for me.'

Eventually Mickey gave in. As soon as he conceded, Heffo stubbed the cigarette out. 'Look, that's great Mickey. They'll be happy to hear that.'

And he was gone. Out the door like a shot. Heffo wasn't going to wait around for Mickey, or give him any time to change his mind!

Down Mickey slumped in the chair.

How has he managed to twist my arm?

Mickey didn't have long to ponder that question. He heard the door swing open seconds later. In came the girls. And it suddenly dawned on him what had happened. The whole evening was a set-up!

Irene walked in, and the first thing she said was… 'Was Kevin here?'

Mickey replied that she knew full well who had been in the house.

'I didn't. I'm only guessing by the cigarettes piled up on the ashtray in the middle of the table.'

His wife pleaded ignorance.

Irene never admitted it.

Kevin Heffernan never admitted it. 'But it was definitely arranged,' Mickey says. 'He had left within minutes of me agreeing to go back for another year, and Irene was likely waiting outside until he left.

'For all I know, Heff could have bought them tickets for the concert that evening, so they would vacate the house.

'Come to think of it, I have no idea if there was even a concert at the Point Depot that night at all!'

◄◄◆►►

TOMÁS 'MOSSY' QUINN

He came in, and just brought a freshness.

The training was tough, but it was really enjoyable. It was all with the ball. And he probably just challenged us in ways that we hadn't been before.

In 2006, we kind of left that behind us. And we probably didn't have enough, a mixture of experience… we didn't close it out. We were by far the better team, but we left them in the game, and they got a couple of points late on. And it was a sickener.

In hindsight, it worked out because we won the All-Ireland on the back of the following year's championship. I don't know if we would have done that in 2016 if we'd have won it. But it was a sickener.

And Mickey found that tough. I know he took that one tough, and was contemplating whether he'd come back. But it was probably the freshness, and just his unique way of speaking to people and getting the team together [that stood out].'

◄◄◆►►

ST VINCENT'S HAD FALLEN short in 2006. Once Mickey had signed up for another year, he needed to put some things in place for the coming year.

First things first, he needed to retain one of the most experienced players. Initially, Pat Gilroy was as adamant as Mickey Whelan that he wouldn't be involved in 2007. But Mickey managed to pull the same trick Heff pulled on him.

However, by that stage Pat was moving into his late-thirties. Though primarily a midfielder, Mickey opted to put him up full-forward for that season. And it worked a treat. His experience was key at the edge of the square, and he brought Mossy Quinn and Brian Maloney into the game either side of him.

He also popped up with some crucial scores, bagging 1-1 against both Portlaoise and Tyrrellspass in the Leinster Championship in the winter of 2007.

He was like a new recruit onto the team, and he energised those around him.

◄◄◆►►

PAT GILROY

He got permission from my wife behind my back for me to continue! When he asked me, I said, 'I'll have to check with Yvonne if I can play another year'. When I went home, she said, 'Oh yeah, of course you can!'

We had just discovered that we had a baby on the way, so I was thinking that was very relaxed from Yvonne. I thought she would have expected me to be at home more. My dad had recently passed away, and I was very upset over that. The football was a great release from all of that.

She was grateful that Mickey came to her, because I was probably moping around at home a bit. It worked out well in the end. The decision was made without me!

But that's the way they operate… they're a different breed, the likes of Mickey and Heffo. They always thought outside the box. They were always very thoughtful about the families, or the people who do make the sacrifices.

When you're playing or managing, you're not making any sacrifices. You're enjoying it. It's your family that get left behind. My wife had to pick up the slack a lot of the time at home and with the kids. So Mickey would be very cognisant of that, and always recognise people in that situation and be very respectful of them.

◄◄◆►►

THE OTHER TWO new additions that season were Brian Maloney and Pat Kelly. Two Mayo natives, who had played in the 2004 All-Ireland final.

After 2006, Mickey thought they weren't far away, but the team needed the final few percentiles.

After training one night, he said as much to Shane O'Hanlon, one of his selectors. The management team always retired to the clubhouse for a cup of tea and a bit of craic, as well as to discuss the team.

'We need another couple of players to get over the line,' Mickey said.

'What about the two Mayo boys?' Shane asked.

'Mayo boys? Which Mayo boys?' This was the first Mickey had heard of them.

'There are two lads that wanted to join Vincent's. They're from Mayo!' Shane explained.

'Well, are they any good?'

'They played in an All-Ireland final!'

Mickey's ears immediately shot up. 'Get me a phone number!'

Mickey thought Shane was going to go away and it would take a few days. But Shane was able to call somebody to get a contact within minutes.

It was 11pm, but Mickey chanced ringing them anyway.

A woman answered.

'Is Brian Maloney there please?'

'Who's speaking? Okay… I'll get him for you'.

'C'mere, my name is Mickey Whelan…'

On the line, Brian explained that both himself and Pat Kelly had been at the county final, and had seen Vincent's play. They were looking to join a club in Dublin, as the commute home to Mayo was too far.

'Can I go down and see you? Can I go down and talk to you now?' Mickey asked.

Despite the late hour, Shane O'Hanlon and Mickey jumped in the car for the short trip to Maloney's apartment.

'We have the whole thing organised,' Brian Maloney explained. 'Our club has told us we can have the transfer on Monday.' This was a Thursday night.

After jumping through a few hoops, the two players managed to get their transfers through to Vincent's. And the pair played starring roles in Vincent's second-ever All-Ireland Club Championship title.

Despite moving home a few years later, the pair of Mayo men still come up to see Vincent's championship matches.

'Once they were St Vincent's men, we treated them as such.'

Tragically, just before the All-Ireland final against Nemo Rangers in 2008, Pat

Kelly's father passed away. Just before he died, he insisted that Pat should play the match at Croke Park on St Patrick's Day.

So, Pat togged out for Vincent's, under undoubtedly difficult circumstances. The funeral was the next day.

There were big celebrations out at the club that night, toasting that second All Ireland success. But Mickey told the team that the management had organised a bus to Mayo early the following morning. No matter what, they were going to go down to the funeral to pay their respects.

'There might have been a few sore heads heading down that morning! Half of them were knackered, and I'd say some hadn't even slept. But it was important to be there for a teammate at such a time, especially after he had togged out the previous day.'

Both Pat Kelly and Brian Maloney proved to be magic for St Vincent's that year.

'When we had them on board at the start of the 2007 season, and Gilroy was staying on, it meant we now had the final pieces of the jigsaw in that Vincent's team; we were already working with a talented group. We had some key players for Dublin, and some who would go on and have stellar inter-county careers.

'I had worked with Ger Brennan on the Dublin minor team in 2003… when we reached the All-Ireland final, but lost to Laois after a replay.

'I made him centre-back. He was a midfielder coming all the way up, but I figured he was better suited to centre-back. He was great for us.

'I was also managing the St Vincent's under-21 team, and knew there were players coming through. Diarmuid Connolly was beginning to make a name for himself. I wanted to take the under-21s and the seniors. I worked really hard with the '21s'. That was my plan, that the good ones would move straight up. We won the under-21 title in 2004.

'The majority of them came onto the senior squad and ended up winning a couple of club All-Irelands. I remember one of the first nights we took that group for training. I sat down with the selectors for a cup of tea, and saw the team coming into the club.

'One of the mentors said to me, "I don't think we have a whole lot there to work with".

'I think we do, I countered. And the reason I thought so was all the young fellas had walked in the gate together. They arrived as a group.

'It may have been a small thing, but I figured these guys were tight. A good number of them made it through to the senior squad.'

◄ ◄ ◆ ▷ ►

NIALL MOYNA

Mickey asked me to get involved with St Vincent's. So I became a selector on the team. And we were also involved in the under-21 team at the time.

The under-21s played the Vincent's senior team in a challenge game one evening. I remember sitting up in the bar that night, and Mickey turning around and saying to us, 'You know something? See some of those under-21s out there? There are eight or 10 of those that are going to be on the senior team. We're going to win the Dublin Championship within two years.'

We won the All-Ireland within three! I didn't see it. Nobody saw it. He just saw there was the nucleus of a team there. He has that unique ability to see things that other people don't see.

◄ ◄ ◆ ▷ ►

THE FIRST ROUND of the 2007 Dublin Senior Football Championship saw St Vincent's up against Kilmacud Crokes. They beat Vincent's 3-7 to 1-7 at Parnell Park.

Two weeks later, Vincent's overcame Thomas Davis in the backdoor to recover.

Wins over Naomh Barróg, Na Fianna and Whitehall Colmcilles followed, before they qualified for the semi-final. Crokes were standing in their way once again.

◄ ◄ ◆ ▷ ►

TOMÁS 'MOSSY' QUINN

One of my big memories working under Mickey, going through that championship… Kilmacud were one of the best teams in Dublin at that time.

Paul Griffin was probably their main defender. And then they had the likes of

Darren McGee, Liam Óg Ó hÉineacháin… they'd a bunch of brilliant footballers.

And they were brilliant. They had won the championship in 2004 and '05… they had beaten us a couple of times.

In 2007, we beat them in the semi-final. Going into it, they (the management) had obviously watched a video and Paul Griffin was instrumental in whoever they had beaten beforehand, in terms of driving out of defence, winning a load of ball… excellent defender.

I remember Mickey saying, 'Look this guy is probably going to pick you up, I want you to go way out to the corner and leave space for others'. When he said it to me initially, I was like… 'Hang on, if I'm out there, and he's out there with me… that means I'm not doing anything!' There was a sense of… Do you think he's good enough to do that to me?

It was only when I did it, that I found myself in more space, and we created more space. It actually worked well. And I probably looked at the game a little bit differently that day. Paul had less of an impact defensively for them. And as it went on, he wasn't sure whether to stand out beside me. Sometimes he'd hedge his bets and I'd get onto the ball. And I remember thinking after the game… That was smart.

◄ ◄ ◆ ► ►

ST VINCENT'S BEAT KILMACUD, 2-11 to 2-9.

Tomás Quinn scored 1-6 (0-3 from play), while Brian Maloney scored 1-1. St Brigid's were next up in the final. By this stage, there was pressure. The club had not won a county title since 1984 when Mickey Whelan was also the manager.

That victory in 1984 was the club's 24th in the space of 36 years.

It was time to end the drought.

In truth, Vincent's were winning the game reasonably well. Brigid's got a goal late in the game, which put some gloss on the scoreboard. But it was a deserved win, 0-12 to 1-7.

For a lot of clubs, a county title is the ultimate aim. *The end goal.* But given the Vincent's pedigree they weren't going to rest on their laurels.

There was a Leinster Championship campaign ahead.

Mickey said to them, 'We are going to start training at 7am'.

One of the players replied, 'I can't… I won't make it to work on time!'

'Fine,' Mickey said. '6am it is!'

He had managed Vincent's for their last county title 23 years beforehand, and they had gone all the way to the All-Ireland final. They were unlucky not to beat Castleisland Desmonds that time. They lost 2-2 to 0-7!

The game was in Tipperary Town. Vincent's had dominated them all over the field, but conceded a goal in the last minute. A defender running back knocked the ball past the goalkeeper and into the net with a couple of minutes to go.

And then, Desmonds got a sideline ball, basically in the corner, and they kicked it into the square. It went into the net.

It was a shattering loss for everyone.

But it was still a continuation of a golden period for the club. In 1981, St Vincent's were celebrating their 50th anniversary. The club had failed to regain the county title after 1977, but huge stock was placed in that season given the year's significance to the club. Mickey Whelan was asked to take charge. But they had a significant number of dual players. The hurlers were also strong, and would be in the reckoning for the county title.

Mickey did not want the dual players getting pulled and dragged, or doing the same running drills twice in the one week – once with the footballers and once with the hurlers.

So he decided that the two teams did all their physical and running sessions together. On the weeks there would be hurling matches, the footballers would be down numbers. And vice-versa. It was a tough balancing act, but the players appreciated not getting dragged in two different directions.

St Vincent's ended up winning the double.

◄◄◆►►

BRIAN MULLINS

When Mickey took the reins, he was a natural for it. In the late 70s… after 1978 and '79, the Vincent's efforts went downhill a little bit.

I was out of the country, living and studying in New York when Mickey took over the senior team with a large batch of younger players.

The key moment in that initial management spell was the fact that St Vincent's were celebrating their 50-year anniversary in 1981. I wasn't involved. But I know enough from what I hear to know that he coached and trained the team in a way that he was well capable of, and was reflective of what he contributed to the earlier spell under Kevin's stewardship of the county in the mid-70s.

I came back to Ireland in 1982.

For me, I was close enough to Mickey to know that at times he was well capable of introducing novelty.

One thing that would stand out from that time was we did a winter series of stamina training, which involved training on Dollymount beach. A lot of the younger fellas on the squad were quite aghast and challenged by having to drive down on a winter's evening to a dark and deserted beach, and under headlights of cars run the length of the beach as a warm-up... and then do a series of drills up the sand dunes.

It made men out of a lot of young fellas who would suddenly realise they were playing adult sport... there was hard work involved in preparing. He deliberately would have decided on that as a venue to test fellas' willingness to go the extra mile.

◄ ◁ ◆ ▷ ►

OVER 20 YEARS on from the Castleisland defeat, Mickey Whelan was determined they would go one step further this time around.

The first round of the Leinster was two weeks later against the Meath champions, Seneschalstown. The team took a slight break after the county final. There was celebrating to be done. And they played a bit of golf in the interim, before knuckling back down to business.

It was a tough match, finishing in a 0-11 to 1-8 draw.

When the referee blew the full-time whistle, Mickey knew he had a problem.

The replay would be the following weekend. But Mickey had committed to travelling to America, as he was being inducted into the Westchester Community College Hall of Fame, for his sporting achievements there over 30 years earlier.

He had already agreed to go back, and had paid his fare. So, he went over, also because his daughter was in college over there, and he wanted to meet her at the same time. So, instead of being on the sideline in Navan, Mickey was over 5,000km away! He was a nervous wreck. A friend of his was giving him the scores.

Vincent's were winning by four or five points. It was suddenly down to three. Two. The nerves!

'I was then told it was full-time. The lads eventually pulled through, 1-12 to 0-10. Talk about being relieved! Funnily enough, I wasn't the only person following one of our matches intently Stateside during that campaign.'

On St Patrick's Day 2008, Bertie Ahern – Taoiseach at the time – was over in Washington DC for the customary visit to the White House, armed with a bowl of shamrock. Bertie had been following Vincent's progress throughout, given St Vincent's was in his constituency.

Bertie couldn't make it to Croke Park on Paddy's Day for the final against Nemo Rangers, as he had a date with U.S. President George W Bush.

Bertie since told Mickey that he had an aid running in and out to him during the meeting. The First Lady Laura Bush asked at one point, 'Is everything alright at home?' She was clearly alarmed by the aid going back and forth, whispering in the Taoiseach's ear. Bertie Ahern told her that his team was playing a big match back in Ireland. 'I'm getting the scores!' he explained.

Apparently when news filtered through of the one-point win, George W passed on his congratulations! Bertie had written Mickey a nice letter, lauding the team's achievement after the Leinster title earlier that season:

Dear Mickey,

Just a short note to send you my heartiest congratulations on the Leinster title. I saw you on the sports news last Sunday and you looked like a very proud man and rightly so. It has been a great season for St Vincent's and the club have certainly brought huge excitement to GAA circles here in the capital.

You deserve great credit for the leadership you have given to many of the young players, not to mention the seasoned campaigners in the squad. I know they will be training hard for the semi-final. You might pass on my congratulations to all of them.

I hope your student life is still going well in DCU, and I enjoyed our chat out there recently. That is a very exciting project you have taken on and I look forward to seeing the results. I wish you, Irene and all the family a very Happy Christmas and best wishes both on and off the pitch, for the New Year.

With my very best wishes,

Bertie.

◄◄◆►►

BERTIE AHERN

I followed Mickey's career closely and stayed in touch with him throughout the years. In fact, I attended the 1963 All-Ireland final when I was 12. I was up in the Canal End with my brother Noel. It was a big deal for me attending that All-Ireland final, and I vividly remember Mickey's performance that day.

When he came back from the U.S. in the 70s, his coaching techniques were revolutionary at the time. It didn't work out for him when he took over as Dublin manager, we just didn't have the players at the time. But he was big enough to come back in with Pat Gilroy a few years later, and they got the whole thing moving again in 2009, '10 and '11.

But I fondly remember that St Vincent's All-Ireland win in 2008. I did 11 of those St Patrick's Day trips to the White House. But the thing that killed me was I always missed the matches in Croker on Paddy's Day! People would think you love being over in Washington DC and all these meetings, but I always missed the club finals.

Particularly that one, because Vincent's were in it. I live in the Marino parish, so that's the GAA club down the road.

U.S. President George W Bush was wondering what was so urgent, when I was keeping up to date on the match! After the meeting, I made a phone call to the guys at Croke Park. I remember speaking to Brian Mullins and Mickey from the White House, and was delighted to congratulate them!

◂◂◆▸▸

THERE WAS NO let-off after Mickey got back from America. No time to sleep off the jet-lag! Portlaoise, who had won the Leinster Championship three years previously, were coming to Parnell Park.

Vincent's beat them well, 3-13 to 1-8.

They followed it up with a 2-8 to 0-7 victory over Tyrrellspass in the Leinster final. The team were going from strength to strength. The young guys were becoming physically stronger, and having more of an impact on the field.

Kelly and Maloney were growing into their roles, the latter being a constant threat in the inside forward line. But after the Leinster final, the team was facing into a two-month lay-off before the All-Ireland semi-final against Crossmaglen Rangers. Mickey decided they would take a break. They had been training hard.

'We're going to break up for three or four weeks now,' he told them.

They went ballistic!

They went to Shane O'Hanlon.

'What does he mean we're not going to train for three weeks? We have an All-Ireland semi-final to prepare for!'

Shane smiled. 'Just do what he tells you!'

CROSSMAGLEN RANGERS WERE kingpins around that time. They were reigning All-Ireland champions, and were fancied to defend the Andy Merrigan Cup. St Vincent's had actually played them the previous year in a challenge game, in which they had been there or thereabouts with 10 minutes to go. Mossy Quinn played brilliantly. But Cross pulled away in the end and won well.

Interestingly, before the All-Ireland semi-final, Vincent's had to complete the 2007 Dublin Division 1 League final. They were up against St Oliver Plunkett/ Eoghan Ruadh.

Crossmaglen knew the game was on, and came down to take a look.

'I knew they would, so I made the decision not to play our full team. I fielded a weakened side, and we lost 2-13 to 1-7.

'Not everyone was happy. But that's what was needed to be done. Every inch was essential. It was all about the All-Ireland Club Championship. We had bigger fish to fry.

'The challenge game the year beforehand had shown that we weren't far off the required standard, and I knew we had improved since then.

'Crossmaglen Rangers won All-Ireland titles in 2007, '11 and '12. And they still don't know how we beat them in 2008! I had seen them play, both on TV and up close.

'Their half-back Aaron Kernan was key to their game. He never went further back past their half-back line He scored a lot for them. He was always their outlet.

'Forwards came back… midfielders came back to defend. But Kernan was always there, ready to break. No matter who won the ball, they kicked it out there because they knew he was there. It didn't matter if they had their back to him, they just drove the ball out there… and he was always there.

'In the build-up to the match at training one evening, I called over Mossy Quinn and Diarmuid Connolly.

'They were going to be key… playing on the same wing.

'Mossy in that challenge game the previous year had played brilliantly against them, so I knew they were going to double-mark him.

'I said, "Mossy, you're going to have two men… you're going to come out to Diarmuid".

'And Diarmuid said, "And I'm to go in?"

Mickey said no!

'You two are going to play left-half forward.'

They were looking at their manager as if he had two heads!

'Mossy, two guys are going to come out with you to shut you down. That's going to be you two against those two, plus Kernan, who will be marking Diarmuid. There's going to be five of you out there, grouped together.

'We're going to play this like a basketball pick. What's going to happen is… balls are going to be coming down to you. But you're going to step out across them. Only one of the five of ye can get the ball. Just make sure it's us.

'One of you will step across the opposition, and the other will get the ball. When he gets the ball, you turn on the outside and get down and back… into the space to take the pass.'

It worked like a dream.

Vincent's beat the Armagh side 2-9 to 0-11.

Mossy Quinn scored 1-2, Diarmuid Connolly scored 0-4.

'THEY WERE TWO fantastic players.

'In my view, Mossy retired from Dublin too early in 2012. By that stage, he had built up massive strength.

'He went on to show what he was capable of after his inter-county retirement, helping Vincent's to another All-Ireland club title in 2014. In my mind, he was the best club forward in the country at that time.

'We made him captain on that team in 2007/2008. That's not a decision we made lightly. We have always selected captains very carefully.

'Diarmuid could do anything. A brilliant hurler too. I'd say he could have taken up any sport and succeeded.

'When I was in charge of St Vincent's, I also insisted on taking the under-21 footballers. I didn't want the hassle of going back and forth to a separate manager, negotiating which players would be training with which teams.

'We got to the county final in 2004. Diarmuid was a minor at the time. We were playing against St Brigid's, who were coming back at us late on. I turned to Diarmuid, who was in the forwards, and told him to go out to midfield.

'You have to win every ball here now!' I told him.

He asked who he was swapping places with?

'Nobody! If your man follows you out… fine. If he doesn't, you will have freedom in the middle of the field.'

Connolly went out to midfield and he caught the next two kick-outs. He was fouled for one, and Vincent's scored from the free. He caught the next one and put it over the bar. He won the game in two minutes.

'From a very young age, it was clear he would go on to be great.'

MICKEY HEARD LATER, when some of the Vincent's lads were in Australia on an International Rules trip, that the Crossmaglen players were still asking, 'How did you beat us that day? What happened there?'

They couldn't figure out what trick had been pulled.

On St Vincent's went to the All-Ireland final, where Nemo Rangers were waiting. Aristocrats of the All-Ireland Club Championship. Not that Vincent's were lacking pedigree; they had beaten Nemo in the 1976 semi-final.

'We knew we were playing another great team.

'I kept our lot confident, and worked them hard. After we got over Crossmaglen, we just knew we had to keep those confidence levels and playing standards.

'Gilroy was a big player in that. When we let a ball into him… Connolly, Maloney and Quinn were coming in as well. And we got goals against Crossmaglen. Most clubs didn't do that.

'On the morning of the All-Ireland final, all the young kids, every kid who was a member of Vincent's with their parents, all walked down to Croke Park.

'It was majestic to see them. We were passing through on a bus. It was a moving moment.'

Vincent's dominated the first 10 minutes against Nemo, and should have pulled further ahead. Connolly hit the upright after bursting through the middle. There were a couple of goal chances that they didn't take. But then Vincent's got a bit of a lead.

Nemo came back, but Vincent's held on for a 1-11 to 0-13 win. Mossy Quinn scored 0-7, five coming from frees.

◄ ◄ ◆ ▷ ►

PAT GILROY

That All-Ireland title in 2008 was a massive achievement for Mickey.

Up to 1984 they had won two out of every three senior championships they entered. Then we went 23 years without a county title.

To win a Dublin Championship was a massive achievement from where the club had fallen. We were Division 2 only five years before that. For him to take it on and win an All-Ireland club was an incredible achievement, because we came from nowhere. Four years before it, we were struggling to stay in Division 1.

He got a hold of the team, won an under-21 championship with most of them and blended them into the senior team. It was inter-county training. We'd be training for two and a half hours in the summer.

He brought the fitness level of that group right up… we were way fitter than anyone in Dublin. Our football was excellent as well. We played a good style. He coached so many of the skills. We had so many advantages too.

At that time, we barely even had one player on the Dublin team. Up to that, only Tomás Quinn and Diarmuid Connolly were getting a look-in. Eventually Ger Brennan, Paul Conlon and Michael Savage came through as well.

He did an incredible job blending the old and the young.

◄ ◄ ◆ ▷ ►

AFTER WHAT HAPPENED when he was in charge of Dublin 10 years beforehand, Whelan had every right to be a proud man managing a team that was winning on the national stage. But, for Mickey, it was never about the men on the sideline… it was about the boys and the men out on the field. The glory was theirs.

'That year, we had come from virtually nowhere. The likes of Portlaoise, Crossmaglen and Nemo were competing in the provincial and All-Ireland Championships nearly every year. We probably came across as a bolt from the blue. They didn't know as much about us.

'But those teams likely did their homework, coming to watch us play.

'I'm not into that as a manager. When you go to a one-off game to watch a future opponent, one particular player could play above themselves. The star player could have an off-day. You could get a false picture quite easily, and focus on the wrong aspects.'

◄◄◆►►

SEÁN BOYLAN

The St Vincent's display in the All-Ireland final that day was incredible. The display personified everything that Mickey Whelan believed in, and everything he is about in gaelic football.

Diarmuid Connolly, Ger Brennan… all of these players singing off the same hymn sheet. It was magic.

NIALL MOYNA

That journey with St Vincent's was redemption for Mickey, after what had happened during his time as Dublin manager. I was living in America at the time of that whole debacle with Dublin. So I do not know much about it.

But I think what hurts Mickey is that they all come out now and tell us that he was ahead of his time. But they didn't say it then. And that really hurt him, and he felt he had something to prove.

The sad thing about it was, he did not care one bit about what criticism they were throwing at him. He couldn't care less. But it was how it affected his family. His family has always been his pride and joy.

He was hurt. He had given an awful lot to the GAA in Dublin. He was certainly way, way ahead of his time.

Mickey felt there was unfinished business. Vincent's had not won a championship in years. It's not as if Mickey took over that year to prove anything to anyone. Everyone knew that Mickey was the godfather of Irish coaching. And he was certainly vindicated following that 2008 All-Ireland Club Championship title.

PAT GILROY

Playing under Mickey, I grew to learn that he never missed a trick.

When I was getting older playing for St Vincent's, Mickey suggested I cycle to training each night, to give myself a proper warm-up. I was busy with work, and wouldn't always have the time. But I didn't want to let Mickey down.

So I used to throw the bike into the boot of my car, and drive up to the estate beside St Vincent's.

I would then throw water over myself, and cycle into the club.

One evening, Ger Brennan saw me taking the bike out of the boot around the corner.

'Whatever you do, don't say anything, it would undermine the whole thing!' I told him.

But on the night we won the All-Ireland, Ger spilled the beans to Mickey.

Mickey just laughed. 'You found out then, Ger? I saw Pat doing it on the very first night he pulled that trick. If that eejit wants to do that, let him do it!'

The St Vincent's team with the Dublin, Leinster and All-Ireland trophies 2007/08.

« CHAPTER 4 »

WAS THE ST VINCENT'S run to the 2008 All-Ireland Club Championship a catalyst for the ensuing success with Dublin?

It certainly looked to be that from a management team perspective, as Mickey Whelan joined Pat Gilroy's coaching ticket.

Down through the years, a strong St Vincent's has often led to a strong Dublin team. In truth, before the Marino club came to the fore, GAA was a 'country' sport in the capital.

Historically, it wasn't a *Dublin* game until Vincent's came onto the scene.

The capital was mostly soccer. Boys played soccer on the streets growing up. It was not a gaelic games stronghold. Also, there was more hurling than gaelic football in Dublin, but they were probably all country lads playing for Dublin teams with the small ball.

Most schoolteachers weren't Dublin people either. It was a Kerry man that dragged Mickey and Paddy Holden out to play for the school in gaelic football. Mickey had never played GAA until he was 12 or 13.

THERE WERE SIGNIFICANT outside influences in clubs, with players coming in from different counties. That was the case with Clanna Gael. There were maybe five or six Dublin lads, but the majority were from elsewhere, living in the capital for college or work.

Clanna Gael weren't the only club like that. Faughs were heavy-hitters in hurling and were the same. UCD always had outsiders. Players from as far away as Kerry would feature in the Dublin club championship.

Mickey's father would sometimes bring him to Croke Park when he was a boy to watch club games, and he would see for himself.

His dad was a soccer man, but would follow Vincent's. They would go to the matches together. St Vincent's began to change the 'country game' narrative. In many ways, they were the 'Dublin' club in the 50s and 60s.

The inter-county success changed how GAA was viewed in the capital too. Crowds grew in line with the All-Irelands in the 50s and 60s, and even further in the 70s. But that was for the big inter-county games in Dublin – it was not reflected at club level, and that is still the case. Parnell Park is never full for a county final. The crowds are small compared to club games in other counties.

Going back to the 50s, St Vincent's backboned the county set-up. Indeed in 1953, Dublin won the National League with 14 of the starting team hailing from the Marino club.

It was not quite that level of representation when Pat Gilroy and Mickey took over in the 2009 season, but Mossy Quinn, Diarmuid Connolly and Ger Brennan were among the players on the county squad.

However, when the new management team came in, they were not interested in anyone's reputation. They set out to find the best group of players in Dublin, rather than merely inherit a group from previous management teams.

If that happened to be the same 20 lads that were there beforehand, well and good. But Gilroy, Whelan and Co. wanted to give a fair crack of the whip to everyone who deserved a chance.

The key was to spread the net as wide as possible.

'WE BROUGHT TOGETHER as many players together as we could, and made four teams for an in-house blitz.

'The key was that myself and Pat would not be managing any of these teams… we were there merely to observe.

'The four groups were divided into north, south, east and west from the county, with the idea being each side would represent the best players from those areas.

'We didn't have a huge amount of input into picking the original four squads, but if we saw that someone we were impressed with on the club scene was omitted, we would certainly recommend them.

'So, when these 15-a-side matches were taking place, Pat, Paddy O'Donoghue and myself, and later David Hickey, would span out to keep an eye on proceedings. We felt it important not to watch the matches together. We would stand on our own, on opposite sides of the field, and then swap positions halfway through a match.

'The logic behind that was we would get different perspectives. If we were standing alongside one another, we might all see the same aspects, and equally miss similar things.

'After the match, we convened and compared notes. Pat might have highlighted one player I didn't particularly notice, and vice-versa.

'We felt it was an important exercise. We wanted to send out a loud message that reputation was irrelevant. It didn't matter how many Leinster titles you had won in recent years, or if you had been an All Star.

'We wanted to find players who ticked our boxes.

'That was a lesson I had learned when I was manager in the 90s. Joe McNally was supposedly *washed up* and his inter-county career was over, but I brought him back in and he did a brilliant job for us.

'So we selected a large number initially, and collated our different opinions. From there, we whittled it down to 70, and told the rest that they might get a chance down the line... to keep doing the business at club level and we might come calling.

'From there, we brought them into training for the initial few training sessions, before narrowing it down even further to 35 or so.'

◄ ◄ ◆ ► ►

IT WAS A somewhat different experience to Mickey's own as a younger man, when he first joined the inter-county team. But then again, some principles always remain the same.

He had missed out on the county minor team. Nonetheless, he kept his head down. That was not going to deter him; if anything, it made him even more determined to succeed.

As a minor, he was playing good football with Clanna Gael's second team, but had not yet made the breakthrough to the senior side.

The reason he was playing for the second team was because Clanna Gael had won the Intermediate Championship. Once you won that, you couldn't play in intermediate again. Clanna Gael had a very strong senior team. So they put the players that couldn't play into the second senior division.

That's how Mickey Whelan was playing second division senior when he was still a minor.

ONE NIGHT, AROUND that time, Mickey was out at a dance at the teachers' club where they used to socialise. They were standing to the side, chatting away. Tom Long, a Kerry footballer and a member of Clanna Gael, pulled Mickey aside.

'Hey Mickey, how are you doing? I see you're playing well with the intermediates,' he said. 'Why would you not play for the seniors?'

Mickey was a bit taken aback.

'That's my ambition… to play for the senior footballers. I'd love to,' he replied.

'Really? It was my understanding that you said you didn't want to play for us.'

The senior management must have enquired about Mickey. Maybe the second team's coaches felt he needed another year at that level. Or maybe they just wanted to keep him, in order to give themselves as good a chance as possible to win their division!

Mickey had told Tom, 'That's my dream… That's what I want to do!'

'Oh, so you'll play for us? That'll be it… you'll be playing for us so in that case.'

They let Mickey play the next Sunday with the intermediates, but that was the last Sunday he togged out with them.

He was up training with the seniors after that.

'IT WASN'T LONG until my buddy Paddy Holden and I were brought into the Dublin senior squad at the same time. It was at the end of 1958. Dublin had just won the All-Ireland Championship, but were adding a few players to the panel ahead of the new season.

'I had no involvement in the 1958 All-Ireland win, and that's one thing I'd like to clear up in this book.

'I've often seen in recent years that I've been credited with winning a medal that year. The confusion comes from the team-sheet in 1958 listing an 'M Whelan'. But that, in fact, was Mossy Whelan – a great Vincent's man. He was a great player and a phenomenal person. Generally, he played midfield or half-back. He was not a big man, but a strong hardy athlete. He was a great fielder and he had a great leap on him.

'I can't lay claim to his role in the 1958 All-Ireland win. I was still a teenager, and brought onto the squad for the first time a few weeks later.'

For the first training session, Paddy Holden and Mickey headed over to O'Toole Park in Crumlin after receiving the invite. They had grown up together – Paddy was from Cabra, Mickey from Cabra West. But they had gone to school together in Saint Peter's in Phibsboro and come through the ranks in Clanna Gael.

They were notified to join the panel just off the back of Dublin's 2-12 to 1-9 All-Ireland final win over Derry.

The National League usually started in October back then.

'We trudged into the changing rooms in O'Toole Park. We felt out of our depth, completely in awe of the players already on the squad! But we weren't shy, it wasn't our first encounter with the elite group of players. We had come up against Vincent's in a league semi-final and had beaten them. Paddy was playing centre-back and I was half-forward.

'We were welcomed in. Paddy had played minor with Dublin. He was a few months younger than me.

'Jim Crowley took us aside. He was a giant in our eyes!'

Crowley said he wanted to give the boys some advice.

They looked at him. Of course, they would listen to any advice from him!

'You have friends, you have pals around where you're living,' Jim began. 'Well, don't forget them. Keep in touch with them, because you're going to be around here for a long time.'

That was a shock.

Jim Crowley was talking about the boys being on the panel for years to come. At that stage they were wondering how long they might survive at that level.

Jim wasn't the only one with gems of wisdom to offer.

Mossy Whelan also called them over. 'You know Norman Allen? Well Norman Allen and I have a system. When there's a bit of a row, if he gets himself into trouble, he has to deal with it.

'But if he's in trouble, I have to watch the backdoor.'

Mickey was standing there thinking to myself... *Backdoor? What's he talking about?*

Mossy continued: 'If Paddy gets into trouble, let him. He has to handle that. But Mickey, you have to mind the backdoor. The easiest way to get a broken jaw is to get a belt from the side when you're arguing and fighting with a guy.

'You're job is to prevent a second guy from striking from the side. Don't let that happen. Just watch the backdoor!'

Going home on the bus, all Paddy and Mickey could talk about was the *backdoor*!

'MY FATHER GAVE me contrasting advice to that of Jim Crowley.

'When the card originally came in the post, inviting me onto the squad, he urged caution.

'He was working on the building of the Pigeon House power station. Occasionally, he worked through the night, supervising the testing of the new boilers being installed.

'On those evenings, I would go across to drop him off his supper. As it happened, he had been working late the night before the card arrived. When the card came I went upstairs to show him what had arrived.

'He read the card and said, "Listen son, there are a lot of good players that never made it".

'I was deflated!

'Just do your best, he told me. Don't expect anything out of it. He didn't want me to be let down. But that didn't happen anyway.'

◄ ◄ ◆ ▷ ►

1959 WAS A hugely significant year for Mickey Whelan, on and off the field.

In gaelic football, he enjoyed a big breakthrough and established himself as a starting player on the Dublin senior team. Off the field, his life was set for a massive moment.

'I used to pal around with two great friends, Paddy Holden from Old Cabra and Johnnie Bogan from my neck of the woods… Cabra West. Both of them were excellent players whom I first met in St Peter's Primary School. The three of us joined Clanna Gael, thanks to our great teacher Maurice (Mossy) O'Connor. He was a loyal Kerryman, and a brother of the great player Gegga O'Connor. I had the great privilege of playing alongside Mossy for a short time when I came out of minor football.

Mossy spent his lifetime teaching and training Dublin schoolchildren and working with the Primary Schools Association.

'One evening in 1958, I was at a dance in the Teachers Club with Johnny and Paddy. They were more confident than me… I was quite shy and reserved.

'They stepped across the floor to ask girls to dance.

'I wouldn't have dared do that in a million years!

'I was standing to the side, talking about football to a few of the lads.

'I got a tap on the shoulder and looked up. I moved to get out of this attractive girl's way, thinking she was looking to get through to someone else.'

Irene McGrath smiled kindly… 'No, you!' she said.

'I can't dance!' Mickey responded.

'My sister is dancing with one of your pals out there… they told me you can dance!' she said, as she gently led me on to the dance floor.

'My beloved Irene.

'The best thing that ever happened to me!

'Interestingly, when I saw her sister, I realised that I knew her. Irene's sister worked in Scaffolding Limited, as a secretary just opposite where I was working as an apprentice.

'Most days, weather permitting all us apprentices would be sitting outside eating lunch and at a regular time each day the secretary would walk past on her way to the company canteen for lunch.

'We'd often see her in the office. We'd be in overalls…. she would be dressed to the nines! As the secretary at the time, she was running the section. So, she'd be meeting business people and all that.

'When Irene took me onto the dance floor and said, "That's my sister!" I laughed.

'They were nothing alike. Irene was fair-headed. Her sister was dark-haired. And she was a step-sister, as I found out later.'

'EVERY DAY, I'M grateful that Irene asked me to dance that evening. It was a match made in heaven, because I would never have had the courage to ask her! She built my confidence over the years. She was a good-looking lady, always with great life in her.

'She was living in a bungalow on the North Road. She lost her father very young, at the age of three. He was a Tipperaryman.

'We began seeing each other. One summer evening about six weeks later, I was meeting up with her to walk down by the Botanic Gardens. And I just said to her, "Listen Irene, I'm going to say something here and you might not like it, but I don't want you seeing anybody else. I want to marry you!"

'She just stood there looking at me!'

Mickey continued quickly. 'I want to marry you, but I wouldn't marry you until I've finished my apprenticeship… until I have a job, and can afford to buy a house.' Mickey said it could take five or six years.

There was no comment from Irene. After a moment, she said, 'Yeah… I'm okay with that'.

She linked arms with Mickey, and they kept walking in the sun.

ON THE FIELD of play, things were panning out just as well.

It started slowly after Mickey was introduced into the Dublin squad. Paddy and Mickey weren't quite thrown in the deep end, but they were being sounded out… *Were the boys up to the task?*

The first game Mickey played was in an O'Byrne Cup final replay. Dublin were playing Meath, away in Navan.

Dublin won that day, with virtually the same team that had won the All Ireland title. But Mickey was thrown into the mix.

'They probably wanted to have a look at me. I remember the nerves.

'I was keen to impress.

'The man I was marking was an excellent half-back, who had won All-Ireland titles with the Royals in 1949 and '54. He was wily and experienced, pulling and dragging out of me the whole time.

'I was very quick as a player, and was trying to break free from him the whole time throughout the game. That was a problem. When I came home that night, my father sat me down. He would rarely talk to me about matches in which I had played, but he had something to say on this occasion.'

Mickey's dad told him he was pulling and dragging with his man all the game.

'No… he was pulling and dragging me!' Mickey protested.

'His job is to stop you getting scores!' his dad stated. 'Your job is to try and get scores… *make* scores. You did alright today, but you can't let yourself get dragged down into an encounter like that.' But therein lay the problem.

'If they keep pulling me, how am I going to get away from them?' Mickey asked.

'Well in that situation, here's what you have to do. The first time the man pulls you, you won't know until he has done it. The next time, let him pull you but win the ball… turn as hard as you can… and hit him in the privates as you turn! In the crown jewels!'

Mickey was looking at his father, uncertainly!

'It's simple, you win the ball… turn into him and… BANG!' his dad continued. 'Then he'll keep the distance. He might give out or charge after you, but he'll think twice about pulling and dragging out of you the next time the ball is coming in.'

It worked!

When Mickey was getting blackguarded during a game, he'd do exactly that. He was a good fielder of the ball, and played midfield a lot for the club as well as for Dublin on occasions.

'When I won the ball, I'd make sure to plant my elbow into the opponent's gut, if he had been hassling me throughout the game.

'The key was to make it look like a natural movement, as you turn after catching the ball. I had to look after myself on the field as a skinny 19-year-old playing senior inter-county football!

'As the weeks passed, I grew in confidence on the team as I established myself. During that time, I began to strike up a rapport with Kevin Heffernan.

'He was a corner-forward. I played on the same wing as a half-forward. Over the course of that first year, he took me under his wing. He was a legend in the game, well established by that point. I'm not sure why, but he gravitated towards me, and was always on hand to offer advice.

'He was a great player; a leader on the team, and a goal-scorer as well. He was more than just a footballer. He had an aura about him.

'Despite him being 10 years older than me, we got on really well.'

On one occasion around then, Kevin contacted Mickey on a Saturday.

'What are you doing?'

'Nothing!' Mickey replied. He was at home. He didn't work on Saturdays.

'I'm going to a funeral in Wicklow,' Kevin said.

'Okay, I'll go with you.'

'I'll pick you up in a half hour!'

Kevin picked him up, and off they went. They were chatting all the way down. When they were passing through Foxrock, Mickey asked about the deceased, who had been a Wicklow footballer.

'Was he a nice guy?'

Kevin replied... 'NO!'

'I was still a young fella, maybe 20 or 21. I said, 'No... no. The man who is getting buried?'

'Yeah... no time for him!' Kevin repeated.

'Jesus, why are we doing going down here then?'

'I respected his football, he was a great footballer... great player!' Kevin Heffernan stated.

That stuck with Mickey, and it summed up Kevin Heffernan.

ONE OF THE first things Kevin Heffernan told Mickey was... 'No hurling!'

Mickey was playing the small ball with Clanna Gael up to minor, but when he joined up with the Dublin squad, he had to commit to football.

The rest of the county squad were under similar instructions, except for Lar and Des Foley. They could do what they wanted! They were well able for the demands of being a dual player. Dublin reached the All-Ireland hurling final in 1961, losing to Tipperary. The Foleys both won Celtic Crosses on the football field in '63.

Des also has the distinction of being the only player to ever win a Railway Cup in both football and hurling on the same day, in 1962.

'There were exceptions of course, when I togged out on the hurling field. When Clanna Gael reached the Junior and Intermediate Hurling Championship finals, they asked me if I could play. I was more than happy to, and Kevin gave the green light.

'I felt embarrassed playing in those games. There were fellas who were training all the time, and I was taking their place.'

IN 1959 DUBLIN beat Carlow and Louth (after a replay) to reach the Leinster Championship final.

That set up a decider against Laois.

◄ ◄ ◆ ► ►

LEINSTER SFC FINAL
DUBLIN 1-18 LAOIS 2-8

I have rarely seen this Dublin side play better football than they did at Tullamore in the second-half.

The injury of John Timmons (midfield) took one of Dublin's forwards from position, yet the selectors made a real find in young Mickey Whelan of the Clanna Gaels club. Playing in Des Ferguson's favourite place on the left wing, Whelan gathered confidence as the game progressed. His solo runs and accurate centres in the second-half helped Dublin's winning score substantially. Dublin look like entering the final again. Kerry are a much-scattered side… Dublin are at their peak, but Kerry will be in close training for the fortnight intervening, and are certain to improve.

Scorers: *Dublin – O Freaney (1-7), M Whelan (0-3), D Foley, K Heffernan (0-2 each), C O'Leary, J Joyce, P Haughey, P Farnan (0-1 each); Laois – M Phelan (2-0), J Kenna (0-5), S Brennan, N Delaney, S Price (0-1 each).*

◄ ◄ ◆ ► ►

THE WIN OVER Laois set up an All-Ireland semi-final showdown with Kerry in Croke Park.

In those days, Dublin did not play on Jones' Road as often as they do now. During that year's provincial championship, they played Carlow in O'Moore Park, Portlaoise and Louth in Páirc Tailteann, Navan… and were back in Portlaoise for the final against Laois.

In the build-up to that semi-final, there was a bit of craic at club training sessions. Tom Long, Gary McMahon and Kevin Coffey were all playing for Kerry. There were a few slags going back-and-forth between the Kerry contingent and the Dublin players.

'We would convene at the stadium in those days. So, I would get the bus, and walk up to the ground. In later years when I owned a car, I drove there.

'Walking out into Croke Park that day was like entering the Colosseum, with over 70,000 fans packed into the stadium.

'It didn't get much bigger.

'It was a dream come true to play those games.

'We were the favourites, as reigning All-Ireland champions. But Kerry can never be written off, and we didn't beat them too often in championship football back in those days.

'I hit the post with a shot, and so did Kevin. Unfortunately, that proved the difference… Kerry won 1-10 to 2-5.

'They were in complete control with 10 minutes to go, leading 1-9 to 0-4. But we got our act together, and fought back. We pulled it back to a point, but Tom Long tagged on a late score to help them over the line.'

◄ ◄ ◆ ► ►

1959 ALL-IRELAND SFC SEMI-FINAL
KERRY 1-10 DUBLIN 2-5

Following a promising opening by Dublin against the wind, Kerry's superiority at midfield gave such regular service to their attack that they ran into a lead that they never lost. For long periods of yesterday's semi-final, Kerry seemed to brush Dublin's champion footballers aside as if they were a lot of schoolboys. Yet Dublin were ever the watchful, efficient footballers that only needed an opening or two to make their mark.

When 10 minutes were left to play, the uneven score read Kerry 1-9, Dublin 0-4. Then came a gallant Dublin rally. Every credit must be given to Dublin for their recovery when all seemed lost. They nearly saved the game in that brilliant session when scoring two goals and two points in a brief period. Here we had flashes from Heffernan, Haughey, Freaney and Whelan which threatened danger to Kerry.

Dublin were within a point of the leaders, but Kerry finished fast and Mick O'Connell placed Long for a clinching point to Kerry.

Scorers: *Kerry – D McAuliffe (1-4), P Sheehy (0-3), M O'Connell (0-2), T Long (01); Dublin – O Freaney (1-3), P Haughey (1-0), M Whelan, K Heffernan (0-1 each).*

◄ ◄ ◆ ► ►

'TOM LONG AND I were great friends. Years later, when I was working in DIT, I put a sign up on the noticeboard about the gaelic football team. There was a meeting for all those who were interested, and in walked one young lad.

'I almost dropped on the spot, he was a dead ringer for Tom. I couldn't believe it. It was as if Tom had stepped out of the 60s and into this room.

'I looked at him and asked him his name.'

Cian Long.

'Long? Are you related to Tom Long by any chance?'

'He's my father!'

'That's why I asked! He was the same build… a powerhouse. And he was a brilliant footballer. He was instrumental as we won a national championship with that team.'

'I NEVER SPARED a thought about it until I sat down thinking about this book, but how strange it was for a 19-year-old competing in such a massive occasion in 1959. For all of that to come so quickly for a player who was unable to even make the county minor squad.

'At the time, all I was thinking about was the next day… the next match… the next competition.

'Only now as I look back, reflecting… *What an experience for a teenager!*

'Nonetheless, we had failed to win the All-Ireland.'

But a Leinster medal was not to be sniffed at, as Mickey was going to find out over the next few years.

The marriage of Mickey's father Frank Whelan and his mother Colleen Drumm. Included is Frank's twin brother Matt who was Best Man.

Irene McGrath and Mickey on their wedding day in 1965.

Irene and Mickey and their children – Cormac, Shane, Colleen, Michelle and Emma – on family wedding days.

« CHAPTER 5 »

1959 WAS THE first time Mickey Whelan would taste defeat to Kerry, but unfortunately it would not be the last.

Fast forward to 2009 and the loss to the Kingdom was a result that dominated Dublin's year. That was unfortunate, as the management team felt they were making real progress before that All-Ireland quarter-final.

The ball was thrown in, and within 36 seconds Colm Cooper had stuck it into the Dublin net. A sucker-punch for sure, but it should not have meant Dublin would roll over. It only got worse from there. A late Conal Keaney goal did little to put any gloss on the end result.

Kerry 1-24 Dublin 1-7.

In the months that followed during the off-season, the management held one-on-one meetings with all the players across three different weekends.

They were intense weekends for Pat and Mickey, but they needed to figure out what the players were thinking. *What was working? What was going wrong?*

One of the questions asked of each of the players was… 'Where did it go wrong against Kerry in the All-Ireland quarter-final?'

Many of the players agreed that the concession of the early goal was a massive set-back. That was true. But Pat and Mickey countered with a follow-up question.

'When is the best time to concede a goal? In the first minute? Or the last minute?'

If a goal is conceded after 30 seconds, there are still over 70 minutes to put things right. If a goal is conceded in the last minute, there is little time to come back from that.

Yes, Cooper's goal was a blow. But the management felt the team should have been able to respond better. Dublin shouldn't have been flattened by it.

After the match, Pat Gilroy famously described the players as... 'Startled earwigs' in their response to the goal. Dublin needed to come back stronger.

Once a panel was decided upon at the end of 2009, it was straight down to business. The National League campaign was all about settling on a team and helping them to find a groove.

It was a three-year project.

Rome wasn't built in a day. There would be lessons along the way.

◄◄◆►►

ALAN BROGAN

Pat probably was a bit of a left-field choice for the Dublin job... it came out of nowhere. But Pat has said himself that he wouldn't have done the job without bringing Mickey Whelan in with him. And I think Mickey brought a lot of credibility to Pat's management team, for the players that were there at the time.

Mickey had a very good reputation in terms of coaching, although his previous managerial career with Dublin hadn't gone too well. Whatever the reason for that, there was a lot of talk that maybe some of his coaching methods were ahead of their time.

After a couple of meetings with the lads, it was clear he knew what he was talking about. Mickey had a great way about him, in terms of getting the most out of fellas. He got instant respect from guys when he came in. Not that he cared what anyone thought!

He just wanted to get the job done.

And that came across very quickly.

Mickey would often let out a roar if he saw someone doing something that wasn't the way it was supposed to be done. That was something that Pat probably didn't do.

Pat managed, and he would occasionally get involved in sessions.

But Mickey would have run all the sessions. Anyone that has trained under Mickey would know that when he lets out a roar, it's unique! He got the most out of fellas. There's no doubt about it.

He wouldn't have been as close maybe to the players as Pat. Obviously there was huge respect there. He kept a little bit of distance between himself and fellas. He had a bit of a serious look about him.

Although underneath it, I think he enjoyed a bit of fun and the craic that might be going on. But he wouldn't let that come across to the lads he was coaching.

Some of the sessions were gruelling.

And some of the time – he obviously knew what he was doing in terms of the sports science side of it – but I think at various stages he decided… I'm just going to run these lads into the ground here to see who can stand up to it. He did a great job with us.

The sign of a good management team or a coach is that after three full years, he still had the full respect of the group.

That's difficult at that level.

If a coach or a manager lets their standards drop, the players will cop on very quickly.

Mickey left after the three years with his reputation enhanced amongst the players he was involved with… that's a testament to himself.

PAT GILROY

I would not have gone in without Mickey, and I don't think the Dublin County Board would have had any interest in me, unless Mickey was coming with me!

It was the two of us, or nothing.

I wouldn't have had the experience or skill-set to take on that job without him. I just wouldn't.

I thought I knew more than I probably did when I took on the job. I learned a lot of hard lessons the first year. But having Mickey and David Hickey there was a huge help. The other selectors too, Paddy O'Donoghue and Paul Nugent, they were all great.

But Mickey was so critical.

The physical preparation of the team… where they got physically in two years from when we took over. They were in great shape when we took over. They were as fit as anyone, but they became twenty percent fitter than anyone.

They could last forever.

In the last 15 minutes of games, they were always beating teams.

They believed as well in their heads that they were probably unbeatable in the last 15 minutes… by the time 2011 came.

Mickey built an incredible base of strength and fitness into them.

His role was primarily around coaching the team. Thanks to my work, I was comfortable doing the background organisation, dealing with the media, dealing with the players and issues outside of football... looking at the bigger picture.

That allowed Mickey to concentrate on football and the skills acquisition. I think he really loved that. A lot of that other stuff, he did it but he didn't particularly enjoy it. I'm not saying I particularly enjoyed it, but I didn't mind doing it.

◄◄◆►►

THAT FIRST YEAR, Dublin had spent the early parts playing challenge matches and the O'Byrne Cup, before a first league match.

Tyrone were coming to Croke Park for the National League opener, and there was no shortage of fanfare around the occasion. It was the 125th anniversary of the GAA. The capacity crowd... the fireworks display and commemorative jerseys which the teams wore in the warm-up aside, it was a valuable run-out against the reigning All-Ireland champions.

It was an early chance for the team to measure itself against one of the best in the country.

Tyrone edged Dublin, 1-18 to 1-16.

Dublin went through that campaign with a mixed bag of results. There were wins over Donegal and Westmeath, draws with Mayo and Kerry, and losses to Derry and Galway, to go with the opening defeat at Croke Park.

Every game, the management felt they were learning about the team and the players all the time.

Coming into a first summer, the one non-negotiable for the management team was that Dublin had to win the Leinster Championship.

Dublin had won the Delaney Cup over the last four seasons. It had become that team's bread and butter. Yes, they had fallen short in the All-Ireland series in each of those summers, but Dublin were still the No.1 team in Leinster!

Had Dublin failed to win the 2009 Leinster Championship, the knives would be getting sharpened. The supporters and the media might pounce, noting how before Gilroy and Whelan and Co. arrived there were no problems winning Leinsters.

Dublin needed to retain the provincial title!

But they were faced with a tricky draw.

Meath were coming to Croke Park for the Leinster Championship quarter-final. As they would learn 12 months later, that was a dangerous fixture.

In 2009, the Meath challenge was safely negotiated.

Conal Keaney kicked five points, and Alan Brogan chipped in with three. Bernard Brogan kicked two. Dublin got over the line.

One headline read... *ONLY TARGET DUBLIN HIT WAS TO WIN THE GAME. The* newspaper continued, *Dublin were emphatically better but the cutting edge of their attack was the least convincing aspect of the performance and consequently the winners had an absurdly meagre two points to show for their 70 minutes of comfortable superiority.*

'A WIN IS a win. And we needed to win that Leinster title.

'Next up in the semi-final was Westmeath. We had beaten them comfortably in the National League, and it was a result that we managed to back up (4-26 to 0-11).

'In the Leinster final against Kildare, we got off to a dream start, scoring 1-3 without reply in the opening exchanges. They came back, however, and we had to dig deep to get over the line (2-15 to 0-18).

'The Delaney Cup was a priority in our mind. Mission accomplished.'

But the All-Ireland series was a different prospect; a stage where Dublin had not delivered in a long time.

In the way stood Kerry. Jack O'Connor's side had recovered from a Munster Championship loss to Cork, with qualifier wins over Longford, Sligo and Antrim.

In the All-Ireland series, it was all-or-nothing.

'We had to drill that into them, and make sure they performed under pressure. The other thing was that we needed to tighten up defensively.

'When we didn't have the ball, we needed each of the 15 players on the field to work together to apply pressure on the opposition and to regather possession. From the corner-forward back to the goalkeeper, everyone was required to work,' Mickey explains.

Initially, however, that wasn't in the nature of all the Dublin forwards.

'From a coaching standpoint, you cannot just tell a player to work harder off the ball. You cannot simply show them either. You need to instil it in their psyche.

'If you gather them around in a huddle and talk for five minutes before letting them back out onto the pitch, it won't stick.

'They would be scratching their heads, thinking… *What did Mickey just say?*

'It might go in one ear and out the other.

'It has to become second nature to them. In order to achieve that, they need to learn it by teaching themselves.'

Implicit learning.

'In training, I put an impediment in their way, but didn't give them a solution. They needed to find the solution themselves. This was achieved by adding conditions to drills or games.

'If we needed our forwards to put in a tougher shift by tracking back and making tackles, we would add a certain condition. For instance, we would make a rule in our games that defenders would need to take two solos before getting rid of the ball.

'Therefore, if a forward was beaten by his man, he had no option but to give up. We would be roaring at him to keep going. He knew that it was worth his while to dig deep, because the back who was rushing out of defence had to hold onto the ball for a few more seconds.

'It forced the forward to dig deep and never give up.

'If a man went by you, you had to get back at him. If I was tackling you, and you went by me, I knew that you had to make two solos. So I bust a gut to get back and make another tackle.

'Once we were satisfied that the forwards were responding and working harder, we removed the condition from the game. But by that stage, it was instilled in them.

'They would never give up, if beaten the first time.

'They would go the extra mile.

'We would then add a different condition, where you can't solo. So now, any player who was in possession had to read the game, make a decision and act quickly.

'We also needed to toughen them up physically.

'In training, we put them into small squares; and set up small possession games. And on the outside, there'd be four players, two on each team, but they couldn't go into the 'pitch'.

'If one of the players in the square got into trouble or was shut down, he could use a teammate on the outside to get it away.

'We would then take one team out and replace them with another, so the men that were very tired would come out and the others would go in. It was one minute on... one minute off.'

'The tight space forced them to think quickly, make the right decisions, and also be able to ship big hits. And most importantly, they were doing all of this when they were nearly wrecked.

'Unbeknownst to themselves, we were improving their reading of the game.

'Those conditioned rules were building them slowly. It was also building their fitness.'

MICKEY THEN REPLACED the footballs with tennis balls at training for the first time.

Why tennis balls?

'Well, firstly it forces you to get in close. With a football, players might stand a bit further back as they try to slap the ball out of an opponent's hands. Whereas with a tennis ball, you need to get right in on top of the man in possession if you are to get anywhere near the ball.

'In those small-sided possession games in restricted areas, they were milling each other. No fouls. But milling each other. Add in the smaller tennis ball, and the physicality went up a few notches.

'Secondly, it improved the players' movement and reading of the game.

'I would get them to throw it and catch it, when practicing our team play.

'If one player had the ball, I wanted two or three men to give him an option.

'Not to stand looking... waiting for him. They made space.

'If he was coming up the left hand side, you got out of the way... you took your man this way, so he could go that way.

'THEY WERE READING and learning at a quicker pace, but didn't know they were doing it! It was implicit.

'If one of our players had the ball, we needed the other 14 to be tuned into where he was going to be next.

'If you tell them, 'You have to do this!' or 'You have to do that!' they're out on the field thinking... *What does Mickey want here?*

'Whereas if you create an environment for them to come up with the solutions, let them go through it, let them fail… they then will learn.

'Players learn best when they are forced to come up with solutions themselves.

'It's like a smaller guy on a team. He knows that he can't go toe-to-toe with the bigger guys, he won't be able to knock the stuffing out of them. So, he adapts his game to compensate. He works around his shortcomings, and maximises his strengths. He finds solutions.

'There are things you can't teach. You have to allow them to learn for themselves.

'The thing was with that Dublin team; Pat and I needed them tackling everywhere. Adding challenges like those in training forced them out of their comfort zones. Over time, it worked a treat.

'By the end of 2011 they were all working in unison. Our levels of work-rate and stamina were higher than any other team, and that laid the foundations for the 2011 All-Ireland Championship win.'

◄ ◄ ◆ ▷ ►

TOMÁS 'MOSSY' QUINN

The role of coach rather than manager definitely suited Mickey, and he was more comfortable with that. Mickey was always at his most comfortable when he was on the pitch, in the middle of drills, challenging guys, throwing new things out, seeing how guys react. He's brilliant at getting you to think differently, to try and engage yourself in training and in practice. So when it comes along in a game, you're not surprised, or you're able to react. That's his skill-set.

He would have come with that credibility of winning that All-Ireland Club Championship in 2008 as well. He was instrumental in that, and we as a club hadn't had success in a long time. He had helped get us over the line.

There were four or five of us from Vincent's.

There would have been a number of players who had dealt with him through Sigerson teams as well, probably five or six from DCU… the likes of Bryan Cullen, Paul Casey, Stephen Cluxton.

He also was involved in the 2003 minors. Mark Vaughan and a few others were on that team. So there were probably enough lads from outside Vincent's that had experience with him, and trusted him. He wasn't starting from scratch.

His work on the training field probably allowed Pat Gilroy to find his feet as a new manager, in terms of... How am I going to deal with the team?... What about the tactics?... What publicly are we doing?

Whereas he knew... Well I've Mickey taking care of the training, I don't have to be worrying about that as well.

I'd imagine a lot of managers go in, and they're almost trying to do everything. And it's tough. Mickey and Pat were great for each other in that sense.

Mickey had the freedom to work on whatever he liked. And while it might have taken Pat a little while, he could focus on the other side of things, knowing Mickey would have us physically right.

◄◄◆►►

OF COURSE, THERE were harsh lessons along the way.

And few were harsher than that 17-point defeat to Kerry.

Cooper's early goal rocked Dublin. But the Kingdom won the match across 70 minutes, not just on one score in the first minute.

The fear for the Dublin management team was... *This is in their heads.*

Were too many lads on the Dublin team thinking that they did not have a right to beat Kerry?

There was only one way to make sure that all of the Dublin players knew they had *every right* to beat their greatest rivals, and that was to beat them.

And then beat them again... and again.

To achieve that, the Dublin team needed to be stronger... physically and mentally.

That All-Ireland quarter-final in 2009 showed that Dublin were still some distance from the full package. But it highlighted where they had to improve.

Mickey was delighted to take up Pat Gilroy's offer of joining his management team in 2009 (left) and they scoured the county looking for new talent.

Their first task was to build greater confidence in the team and allow them to fully believe in their own destiny, though nobody could have dreamed Dublin would dominate the game for a full decade.

Of course, Dublin's year ended up in a crushing loss to Kerry in August of 2009.

« CHAPTER 6 »

RECOVERING FROM A loss to Kerry is not easy. Dublin had spent over half a century with Kerry... *in their heads.*

During the 70s, the rivalry between the two counties was fierce.

Dublin had won All-Ireland titles in 1976 and '77, and had beaten the Kingdom in both campaigns. However, those were the *only* two Dublin wins over Kerry in championship football between 1934 and 2011.

The Dublin-Kerry games in the 70s were brilliant occasions to attend. A packed Croke Park, and two brilliant teams competing at their peak.

Kerry had won so many All-Irelands, and Dublin had not managed to beat them for so long. While Dublin managed to win in 1976 and '77, Kerry had a younger team in that era, they were coming stronger, and they took over then by winning four All-Irelands in-a-row. They were an incredible team.

DURING KEVIN HEFFERNAN'S brilliant reign in the 70s, Mickey Whelan helped out by setting training drills and offering coaching advice. He was never in attendance for the training sessions, but the players knew that he had an input.

Heffo would ask Mickey to set up a few drills, and tweak things from afar. This was even happening when Mickey was in America.

In the run-up to the 1975 All-Ireland final against Kerry, Mickey went down to Parnell Park the previous weekend just to take a look at how things were proceeding. He looked, and he thought to himself… *There's something wrong there!*

After the training session, he went into the changing rooms to look for Heffo, to discuss his observations.

He walked into the old rickety changing rooms in Parnell Park. They were wooden shacks. As he was walking in, he bumped into Tony Hanahoe, who was coming out of the shower with a towel around him. 'How's it going, Mickey?'

Mickey immediately noticed how skinny he was looking. He could see Tony's ribs sticking out. He was skin and bone!

Mickey *saw* the problem.

He met Heffo the next day. This was 10 days out from an All-Ireland final.

They sat down and had a cup of tea.

'Kevin!' Mickey began, 'Don't train the team next week. Just relax them!'

He explained how he had seen Brian Mullins miss one particular catch, and how Hanahoe appeared to be too light. It was a big decision to make, to stop training before an All-Ireland final.

Kerry ended up winning that final, 2-12 to 0-11.

On the Sunday evening, Kevin rang Mickey asking him to come over to his house. The Heffernans were getting ready to head out to the banquet, but the two men chatted anyway.

Mickey knocked on the door and Heffo answered. Before they even exchanged greetings, Heffo said, 'Don't tell me you told me so!' They sat down.

'Why did you tell me that last week? Why did you think that?' asked Heffo.

'They were being overworked… overtrained!' Mickey replied. The old friends continued to talk it out.

It was not long before the National League would be getting underway, in October. Mickey advised doing nothing with the team before the Christmas break.

'But they'll go drinking!' Heffo stated.

'So what?' Mickey said. 'Let them… Kerry will be too!'

Kevin Heffernan still had an uncertain look on his face.

Dublin were playing Kerry in the first round of the National League.

KEVIN HEFFERNAN DIDN'T train his team. He just did one Saturday session. The players, fresh from their disappointment in the All-Ireland final, were all ready to get back into the serious work on the training field. Dublin went down south and beat Kerry, with no training under their belt. Kerry were hard into their celebrations. But Dublin beat Kerry well.

Mickey was in Vincent's clubhouse the night after that game. In came Jimmy Keaveney, having landed back on the team bus. He looked unhappy!

'Mickey, you have that man gone mad… HE'S GONE MAD!' Keaveney said of Heffo.

'What's wrong with you? You had a great win,' Mickey replied.

'He is after telling us that we won't be training for six weeks! He said we're not training now until March. What are we doing? He's going mad!'

'Jimmy, there'll be loads of time… you have to recover. There'll be loads of time.'

Keaveney went off into the back room to have a few pints with the other county players who were landing back from Kerry.

◄ ◄ ◆ ▷ ►

JIMMY KEAVENEY

You go back to when we were training in the 70s and training consisted of a few laps, a few sprints. Mickey was studying in America at the time and, all of a sudden, Kevin Heffernan changed the type of training we were doing.

It was totally new to everybody.

That was all coming from America… from Mickey. Then Kerry copped on to it and Kerry started doing what we were doing. We trained on a Saturday, the day before a match, which was unheard of before.

Mickey would have been a very good friend of Kevin's.

He gave him all these ideas which we thought were crazy at the time. He transferred a lot of his knowledge to Kevin during the 70s.

I played with Mickey… won an All-Ireland club championship and numerous county championships with him. He always had this great love for gaelic football.

He is a total fanatic when it comes to it.

BRIAN MULLINS

We were aware that there was a training science to what Kevin had brought to the routine and to Dublin's preparation for performance. For me as a youngster, I was only 18 or 19 years of age, so it wasn't a surprise to me.

But it was probably a bigger surprise to the older crew in the squad who had been through some number of years of not taking county training too seriously… or training at county level not being too serious or scientific.

For me as a young fella, I was delighted!

The more they threw at you, the more you liked it. Myself and a few others… you could handle anything when you're young and you're enthusiastic.

◄◄◆▷►

ALTHOUGH HIS FIRST season as an inter-county footballer saw him join up with the reigning All-Ireland champions, win a Leinster title and play in an All-Ireland semi-final against Kerry at a packed Croke Park, Mickey Whelan would soon learn that such opportunities didn't come around every year.

In 1960, Dublin did start at a lightning pace.

The Leinster Championship quarter-final saw them pitted against Longford in Mullingar. Longford had beaten Meath in the first round to qualify to play against Dublin. Dublin tore them to shreds.

Johnny Joyce scored 5-3, which remained a record individual scoring haul in championship football up until 2020 when Cillian O'Connor bested it with 4-9.

Kevin, Des 'Snitchy' Ferguson and John Timmons all contributed significantly on the scoreboard too.

The end result read: Dublin 10-13, Longford 3-8.

It's not too often that any team scores 10 goals at that level! It set Dublin up nicely, and they fancied themselves coming into the Leinster semi-final against Offaly. Dublin were in the hunt for a third consecutive provincial title.

Now in his second year on the panel, Mickey felt himself growing in confidence.

After scoring so freely, Dublin were being hyped up. And it was all going swimmingly at half-time when they led 0-7 to 0-5 against Offaly.

However, from there the Faithful County turned it around. They left Dublin waiting on the pitch to start the second-half. They stayed in the dressing-room for longer than the allotted time.

Did that unnerve the champions?

◄◄◆▷►

1959 ALL-IRELAND SFC SEMI-FINAL
OFFALY 3-9 DUBLIN 0-9

The biggest surprise of a surprising championship year was the defeat of Dublin footballers by Offaly in the semi-final of the Leinster Championship at Portlaoise yesterday. The holders were beaten by three clear goals and, on the run of play, Offaly thoroughly deserved the victory.

The winners had a splendid defence... Not a man of Dublin's 15 lived up to reputation. Best of them were Paddy Holden and Liam Quinn. Against a brisk, battling Offaly side who always played strong, robust, but thoroughly fair football, Dublin's 15 had a very bad day.

◄ ◄ ◆ ► ►

OFFALY WOULD GO on to bring eventual All-Ireland champions Down to a replay in the semi-final. Indeed, it would prove to be the first of back-to-back Leinster titles for them.

Mickey and other young bucks on the Dublin team were quickly learning just how difficult winning an All-Ireland title could be.

The Leinster Championship was fraught with danger in those years. There were star players in nearly every county.

Mickey was lucky enough to play with most of them in the Railway Cup. Back then, that competition was a massive deal. During his career, Mickey won an All-Ireland title and four Leinster Championships, but after that he treasured a Railway Cup medal amongst his greatest achievements on a GAA field.

The finals took pride of place at Croke Park on St Patrick's Day.

The beauty of the competitions was that there were great players from various counties that would never get a chance to play on the biggest stage otherwise. If, by the lottery of birth, they were from counties that weren't competing for provincial titles, their talents would not be displayed to big audiences.

These players were every bit as good as players who were winning All-Ireland titles. In some cases, they were even better.

The Railway Cup gave *everyone* a platform to perform on a national stage.

Each squad comprised the best 20 players from right across each province. The prestige associated with the tournament would ensure that. There were often trial games, where the reigning provincial champions would face a 'Rest of Leinster' selection.

'MY FIRST TIME getting selected was in 1962. We qualified for the final against Ulster, after beating Munster in the semi-final. Des Foley had already won the hurling decider earlier in the afternoon against Munster, before lining out on the football final.

'That day at Croke Park marked the first gaelic football match to ever be broadcast on live television. Telefís Éireann had gone on air for the first time a few months prior.

'We beat Ulster 1-11 to 0-11.'

Mickey scored the goal, and as a result he holds the distinction as the first player to ever score a live televised goal in a gaelic football match.

'I remember it well. They had brought me out to midfield at half-time to mark Eugene Larkin from Armagh. I picked up possession and made a run forward. I kept soloing it further and further, and John Timmons was running ahead of me... but away from me. His marker was going with him.

'I kept moving forward, but was hoping John would check back so I could slip it to him. But he just continued forward.

'So I took on a shot.

'Being honest, I was going for a point. But when you're travelling at full tilt and kick a ball, you can get over it too much. I got over the ball to drive it over. But it flew into the top corner... it was a perfect ball, right into the top corner.

'I told the lads afterwards that I was going for a point, but I was happy to take the plaudits!'

The goal proved the difference in a three-point win.

Ulster went on and won seven of the next nine Railway Cups. The reason they were so successful was how well they were prepared. The Leinster team was just selected by the provincial council, and all the players would just show up on the day. Leinster never trained. Whereas Ulster were doing weeks, if not months of preparation. Even though the National League was going on, they were training as well.

'It is a pity to see what has become of the Railway Cup in recent years. When I was playing, the finals would attract tens of thousands at Croke Park. The best players in the country would be on show.

'In recent years when it was held, crowds dwindled to a few hundred.

'It is a shame the competition hasn't returned to its former glories.

'1962 was my first year playing with Leinster. While I never won another Railway Cup, I did play in it with the province for several more years, right up until I moved to America. I only missed one year due to illness.'

THE DEFEAT TO Offaly in 1960 may have sent Dublin crashing back down to earth, but they were hungry to get back competing for silverware.

The following year, they battled back into a Leinster final. First up, Dublin overcame Wexford, 4-7 to 0-7.

One newspaper reported: *Dublin had little trouble in overcoming Wexford in the second round of the Leinster Senior Football Championship at Carlow. They took full control after 10 minutes and never lost their hold on the game. Play was very scrappy throughout, however, and although conditions were perfect, there was little or no classic football. The city men were faster and better coordinated all through and took complete command in the second-half.*

Meath were up next, away in Navan.

It was a hurdle Dublin easily overcame, finding the net four times once again.

◄◄◆►►

1961 LEINSTER SFC SEMI-FINAL
DUBLIN 4-14 MEATH 1-7

Dublin beat Meath in the Leinster semi-final at Navan yesterday because they were faster, fitter men with better positioning sense and the ability to pounce on the loose ball… It was an even match throughout the first-half. The Meath defenders kept Dublin's forwards out of shooting range with the result that Dublin scored only two points from play. These came from centre-field man [Mickey] Whelan, who with Des Foley broke about even with Meath's Keenan and Moore up to half-time. When Keenan was hurt in the second-half, the Dublin pair took command.

◄◄◆►►

OFFALY WERE WAITING in the Leinster final, looking to defend their title.

Dublin were planning on revenge for the previous year, but it didn't quite work out that way. Offaly led 1-8 to 0-4 at the break.

And Dublin were unable to claw back the deficit.

It all kicked off after the match.

◄◄◆▷►

1961 LEINSTER SFC FINAL
OFFALY 1-13 DUBLIN 1-8

A rampant Offaly team sent Dublin's footballers toppling to defeat in a robust, rousing Leinster final.

Tempers were lost often throughout the hour and there were isolated incidents which the referee might have handled more strictly, but it was not until after the match, as some of the players were shaking hands, that the real trouble started.

Dublin and Offaly players became involved in a fracas and this was the signal for about a thousand spectators to rush onto the field and join in a general melee. Some of the footballers were hurt and had to be assisted to the dressing-rooms and only immediate action by the Gardaí prevented a complete riot.

It was a sad sequel to a game that had the crowd cheering at every passage of the play.

***Scorers:** Offaly – H Donnelly (0-6), M Casey (1-2), D O'Hanlon (0-5); Dublin – J Timmons (0-5), M Whelan (1-1), P Farnan, K Heffernan (0-1 each).*

◄◄◆▷►

IT WAS A feisty match, with a bit of niggle throughout.

When Mickey scored his goal, he turned around to run back out to midfield. But one of the Offaly backs flattened him as he was turning.

Naturally, his teammates stuck up for him, and one of them clipped the Offaly back for his troubles! That was the foundation for the row.

When the full-time whistle was blown, that Offaly player was looking to exact a bit of revenge. The crowd was swarming onto the field to celebrate. They weren't looking for trouble.

But a few scuffles broke out amongst players, and it became quite dangerous.

'I was still a young lad at that point, having just turned 22. I remember Kevin Boland – a Fianna Fáil politician and a big Dublin GAA fan – was roaring for people to create a barrier around the players!

'My father materialised over my shoulder, saying he was there to take care of me. Now he was a man who was more than capable of looking after himself. He was a champion boxer in the army in his youth!

'I didn't even know that he was going to be at the match. He told me he never used to attend games, as he felt it could make me more nervous. So he turned up unannounced. I had no idea he was at that Leinster final, until he appeared on the pitch at full-time.

'Once we were safely herded back into the dressing-room, there were supporters roaring in the window too. We eventually got back to Dublin in one piece that evening!

'Even back then, there was always an undercurrent of a rivalry when we played anybody in Leinster. They always wanted to get one over on us.'

When the dust eventually settled after the chaos at full-time, Dublin were out. Another barren year. A Leinster title came early in Mickey's career, but a second was proving elusive.

Fortunately, that all changed the following season.

IN 1962, KEVIN Heffernan and John Timmons dragged Dublin over the line in a hard-fought Leinster quarter-final win over Louth in Tullamore, 1-8 to 0-10.

They had to dig deep again two weeks later, beating Laois 0-13 to 1-8.

Offaly were next in the final. Fortunately, it was a case of 'third time lucky' against them. The decider was staged in Croke Park, and a record crowd of 59,643 attended. Paddy Delaney and Bob McCrea got Dublin's goals, and they won 2-8 to 1-7.

Dublin were provincial champions once again, and were back in an All-Ireland semi-final.

The fact that it was three years since their last provincial success meant the draw rotation for the All-Ireland semi-finals had come full-circle, and Dublin would be facing the Munster champions once again.

Surprise, surprise, it was Kerry standing in their way of an All-Ireland final spot once more.

Unfortunately, it was to be another bad day at the office against Kerry. Mickey was well marshalled by Seamus Murphy, the great Kerry half-back.

DUBLIN ANNIHILATED BY MAJESTIC KERRY.

That was one headline, and it summed up the encounter. Mick O'Connell and Tom Long led the way for an eight-point win, 2-12 to 0-10.

Lining out with Leinster was always a proud moment. Here Mickey is (top) third from left in the front row when they played Ulster in the Railway Cup final in March of 1962. Kevin Heffernan is second from right in the back row. And (below) celebrating with Kevin and teammates with the Delaney Cup after winning the Leinster Championship.

« CHAPTER 7 »

AT THE BEGINNING of 1963, Kevin Heffernan suggested that Mickey Whelan take over the free-taking duties.

Mickey took the frees with Clanna Gael. And he was more than happy to do the same with Dublin.

'Free-takers often talk about processes or rituals. I was never into any of that. I put the ball down on the ground and kicked it. Just looked to put the ball over the bar.

'You use your experience.

'Your brain tells you… *You're going to put this over the bar.* You have to block out the noise and simply put it over.

'As a result of taking frees, my scoring tallies naturally increased.'

Going into 1963, Mickey had four years of championship football under his belt. But with the perils that lay in Leinster, every single summer was like walking across a mine-field.

'Any day you went out could spell the end of your season. We scraped through the provincial opener against Meath at Croke Park that year, in a 2-6 to 2-5 win.'

Kildare were next in the semi-final.

Dublin were 2-7 to 1-5 winners.

Laois were the opponents in the Leinster final.

◄◄◆►►

1963 LEINSTER SFC FINAL
DUBLIN 2-11 LAOIS 2-9

For their courage and resilience alone, Dublin deserved a more flattering margin than two points in their successful defence of the Leinster Senior Football title in a tensely exciting but terrifyingly rugged final against Laois at Croke Park.

But on the run of play, and especially in the last eight minutes the holders were fortunate to withstand a vigorous challenge by a Laois side who had a mighty effort to save the day.

For their survival, and a place in the All-Ireland semi-final against Down or Donegal, Dublin can thank first of all their greater speed and fitness, an intimate knowledge of the pitch, and a crafty attack which at times had the usually competent Laois backs in a whirlpool of panic.

Mickey Whelan's appearance at midfield immediately turned the tide for Dublin in a sector where Tom Browne and George Rankins had made hay. The Clanna Gael man was unbeatable for the remaining 26 minutes and the fruits of his magnificent performance went up on the board in the 41st and 49th minutes when Brian McDonald and Gerry Davey got the goals that shattered the challengers' chances of victory.

Dublin: P Flynn; L Hickey, L Foley (0-2), W Casey; D McKane, P Holden, M Kissane; P Downey, J Timmons; E Breslin (0-1), M Whelan (0-6), G Davey (1-1); B McDonald (1-1), D Ferguson, S Behan.

Laois – P Bracken; T Delaney, M McDonnell, R Millar; J Hughes, L Doran, O Fennell; T Browne (0-1), F Walsh (0-1); D Delaney (0-1), E Dunne, G Rankins; S Price (0-1), N Delaney (2-1), D Byrne (0-4).

◄ ◄ ◆ ▷ ▶

'1963 WAS MY third Leinster title.

'Any provincial medal I won was always brilliant, but falling at the All-Ireland semi-final stage left a sour taste. That year saw us pitted against Ulster champions Down, who had won the Sam Maguire Cup in 1960 and '61.

'With Kerry eliminated in the other semi-final two weeks prior to our clash, the stakes were high.

'It was a scrappy affair… the referee awarded 48 frees.'

1963 ALL-IRELAND SFC SEMI-FINAL
DUBLIN 2-11 DOWN 0-7

What a remarkable year this has been for Dublin. Unfancied in all their games in the Leinster Championship, they were slight outsiders again before yesterday's game; but true to the pattern of their provincial triumph, they rose to the occasion magnificently and had they qualified for the decider on September 22nd by 20 points instead of 10, they would not have been unduly flattered.

The backs again formed the massive barrier that even the fast Galway forwards are not likely to surmount; John Timmons secured almost every ball that dropped in or around the centre, and the forwards, cleverly led by Mickey Whelan, began their relentless bombardment of the Down lines.

Whelan, whose combination of speed and wiles Dan McCartan or Patsy O'Hagan could never fathom, was the inspiration of the forward division.

None of the others reached the brilliant heights of the Clanna Gael man, although Brian McDonald, Gerry Davey and Des Ferguson played important roles in a vastly improved sector.

◄◄◆►►

'REACHING AN ALL-IRELAND final was a brilliant feeling.

'It was a huge occasion, you could sense that from the build-up. But by that stage I understood that these occasions did not come around very often.

'One of the significant aspects that struck me walking around in the parade was just how many were rammed into Croke Park. There were 87,106 in there... the third biggest crowd ever at HQ to this day.

'And that was just the official number!

'I heard later that one of the gates was broken down that afternoon, so hundreds more poured in that weren't accounted for at the turnstiles.'

◄◄◆►►

BERTIE AHERN

I was there in 1963 with my older brother, who lifted me over the stiles.

Those were the days when you were able to go to an All-Ireland final without having to go through the manic hunt for tickets. He sat me up on the big fence that divided the Canal End terrace with the Hogan Stand.

He told me, 'If the fence starts to sway, just stay on top of it. And if you get a chance, jump clear!'

I remember the day well, and Mickey Whelan's performance was a standout memory.

◄◄◆►►

'AT THIS STAGE, I was 24. The size of the crowd did not bother or unnerve me.

'The experience I built up over those few years prepared me for any atmosphere. Going down the country for matches, even if the stadium was smaller, it was just as loud. A lot of the time, the vast majority of the crowd was hoping Dublin would lose!

'If you could play in those places, you could play anywhere.'

If people were complaining about the spectacles of the two semi-finals, there were no such concerns in the decider.

GALWAY GO DOWN FIGHTING IN THRILL-A-MINUTE FINAL.

That was one headline.

It was neck-and-neck all through.

◄◄◆►►

1963 ALL-IRELAND SFC FINAL
DUBLIN 1-9 GALWAY 0-10

Dublin forged their narrow victory by a combination of good fortune, clever tactics and the ability to avail of almost every scoreable opportunity that came their way.

Fortune smiled on the Leinster champions in the shape of a blight of inaccuracy among the Galway forwards which resulted in 12 wides over the hour. In contrast to this Dublin nursed every possible chance, as their negligible total of four wides – all in the second-half – clearly testifies.

The metropolitan officials played their trump at half-time. When the teams appeared for the second-half, Mickey Whelan had moved to midfield, where an off-form John Timmons had given Des Foley only token assistance during the previous 30 minutes.

The effect of this reshuffle was immediate. Whelan matched and occasionally beat

Garrett in the middle. So many men played such a handsome part in the victory that it was not easy to apportion the laurels to those that deserved them most. Mickey Whelan perhaps for his unflinching efforts against John Donnellan in the first-half, more especially for his display at midfield after the interval, is entitled to top the list.

Dublin: P Flynn; L Hickey, L Foley, B Casey; D McKane, P Holden, M Kissane; D Foley, J Timmons (0-2); B McDonald (0-1), M Whelan (0-5), G Davey (1-0); S Behan, D Ferguson (0-1), N Fox.

Galway: M Moore; S Meade, N Tierney, B McDermott; J Donnellan, E Colleran, M Newell; M Garrett, M Reynolds; C Dunne (0-2), M McDonagh (0-5), P Donnellan; J Keenan (0-2), S Cleary, S Leydon (0-1).

◄ ◄ ◆ ► ►

'IT WAS A switch I made in every match that year.

'I would start in the half-forward line, and they would then move me out to midfield in the second-half when the game opened up. John Timmons would swap into the forwards, and I helped Des Foley out in midfield.

'It worked a treat.

'When the final whistle was blown, it was magic. The crowd poured onto the field. We were surrounded within seconds!

'The celebrations were brilliant. What a feeling.

'There was a big function the night we won the All-Ireland. None of the team used to drink, apart from John Timmons. We would go out to the post-match functions and dances, but only ever drank water.

'John was the exception. I remember when I was 19, we were driving back from an away game against Louth which we won. We would never get a bus... we would go in a fleet of cards. Joe O'Hara, a county board official, provided the cars as he worked as an undertaker.

'After matches, we would stop somewhere to get food. But the mentors would like to have a few pints, so they would make sure that wherever we would go for dinner would also sell drink! John would sit with the mentors.

'On this occasion, there were four or five of us in the car. We pulled over at the side of the road, as John discussed with the mentors where we would all be going afterwards.

IT WAS UNDOUBTEDLY Mickey Whelan's best ever season in the Dublin jersey. Some even thought he might be named Footballer of the Year. That was an award introduced in 1958. He was the championship's top scorer that season, getting 1-20 across five games.

But Mickey was pipped to the post by Lar Foley.

It was also the first year of the Cú Chulainn Awards – the precursor to the All Stars.

Immediately it was a big deal.

Three Dublin lads were selected that season… Paddy Holden, Des Foley and Mickey Whelan. Funnily enough, Lar Foley was excluded from the team.

THERE WAS STILL one hurdle to overcome following that 1963 All-Ireland triumph. Dublin had won the Sam Maguire Cup, but they had not beaten Kerry along the way. They did not have long to wait for an opportunity to underline their status as champions, however.

After beating Galway in the All-Ireland final, Dublin immediately thought of their Grounds Tournament semi-final clash with Kerry.

This was a game they felt they just had to win. Going out of the dressing-room in Croke Park that day, the team felt that their All-Ireland success would not be complete until they achieved what no Dublin team had done in a major competition for over 20 years.

Kerry were perhaps the best team Dublin met in 1963.

The performance was typical of that Dublin team. They just didn't know when they were beaten. Dublin gave Kerry an almost unbeatable lead and still emerged victorious. They would go on to beat Galway in the Grounds Tournament final.

◄ ◄ ◆ ► ►

SEÁN BOYLAN

I can't explain how good a player Mickey was. I saw him in 1959. He was magnificent. He was one of the outstanding footballers in the country.

Honest to God, his acceleration… from the minute he took off, he was at full tilt. He had an incredible balance, he could go left or right, he could turn… he could twist, he could fetch his ball… he could win his ball. And he was fearless. He was way ahead of his time. That Dublin team in the late-50s and early-60s had the intelligence of pulling defenders out from their positions and they opened up teams.

Mickey was involved in all of that. He had all of that in spades.

He had an ability, from nowhere, to be in the right position. He didn't always get it, but he made himself available. If you go back to that 1963 final, you had Des Ferguson in full-forward… it was an extraordinary team. Des and Lar Foley were there. But Mickey was the man that made it all tick, more than anyone else. He had that incredible energy.

He never wanted anybody else to do the work for him. It seemed nearly a case of…

'How dare you not trust me to do the work?'

That wasn't being in any way brash or anything like that at all.

He wasn't afraid of winning. He knew exactly how to win.

People didn't realise he was such a big man… and he walked like a soldier. Very proud of who he is… where he is from. They were very important things to Mickey.

What amazed everybody was his longevity. I remember him playing out in Sandymount years later with the club. It was just amazing.

And yet he was the same Mickey Whelan.

◄◄◆►►

IN 1963, CLANNA Gael reached the Dublin county final. They eventually lost to UCD after a replay. In those days, the county champions would nominate the captain of the Dublin senior team.

As UCD were a team of country players, they didn't have anyone from Dublin. But they had the right to nominate the captain for the county team.

UCD chose Mickey Whelan.

'It was an honour to captain the county. It may not have necessarily been something I always strived for, but nonetheless I was grateful to be nominated. I was still a young man, and at that stage I was just delighted to be on the panel!'

Dublin hit the ground running in the 1963-64 National Football League.

In the group phase, they won five of their six matches, qualifying for the semi-final.

They overcame Kerry, 0-10 to 0-9 at Croke Park, to qualify for the 'Home' final against Down. Mickey missed the semi-final due to a knee injury.

It was a 'Home' final rather than a 'final' outright, as New York received a bye to the decider. Not only that, but they would be hosting the winners at Gaelic Park.

It was a huge opportunity.

Dublin won convincingly.

◄◄◆►►

1964 NFL 'HOME' FINAL
DUBLIN 2-9 DOWN 0-7

Dublin, who last visited New York for an exhibition match in the summer of 1956, booked their passage for another trip to the United States next October, when they trounced a ragged Down side in the Home final of the National Football League before a record crowd of 70,126 at Croke Park yesterday.

The All-Ireland champions confirmed their standing as the most powerful combination in current football and indeed enhanced their prospects of retaining the Sam Maguire Cup next September.

Brian McDonald, Eamonn Breslin, Gerry Davey and Mickey Whelan were outstanding in an attack that worked with typical precision once the ball was in plentiful supply. Whelan still shows some slight effects of his knee injury, but he eluded Dan McCartan many times in the last 20 minutes, and might have added two goals to his side's total if he hadn't been blatantly pulled down when racing through the centre on two occasions.

◄◄◆►►

DUBLIN HAD BOOKED their trip to the Big Apple.

It was a perfect springtime campaign. However, dreams of New York had to be parked. The 'final' proper was not scheduled until October.

First up, Dublin had the small matters of Leinster and All-Ireland Championship defences to attend to. They opened up with a straightforward win over Carlow, 1-14 to 1-5. It was followed up with a 0-8 to 1-2 semi-final victory over Laois. Another provincial final beckoned. Dublin had won Leinster, All-Ireland and National League titles. Now it was time to defend them.

But the team was almost burned out. They had been on the road for well over a year. They had won all before them. But it had to end at some point.

Eventually, it all caught up on Dublin.

Coming into the Leinster final, Mickey was informed that he was no longer the captain of the team. St Vincent's had recently won the Dublin Senior Championship for 1964.

Mickey was informed just before the match.

'It threw me, being honest.

'My head was all over the place, and I didn't play well.

'Meath beat us well.'

◂◃◆▷▸

1964 LEINSTER SFC FINAL
MEATH 2-12 DUBLIN 1-7

It was a nightmare outing for Dublin. Perhaps it was just one of those days which all teams encounter at some stage or other. But even at the interval when they were only a point in arrears, they were never functioning with their usual efficiency.

The speed and mobility which played such an important role in their climb to the top has all but been drained by a hectic 18-month campaign, in which they have lost only two games of note prior to yesterday.

The enforced absence of John Timmons disrupted the team still further. And with Simon Behan giving Des Foley little more than token assistance at midfield, they were seldom moving on an even keel.

Meath: P Cromwell; D Donnelly, M Quinn, P Darby; P Collier, B Cunningham, P Reynolds; J Quinn, P Moore; D Carty (0-2), T Browne, J Walsh (0-4); G Quinn, K McNamee (0-3), O Shanley (1-3). Sub: P Mulvaney (1-0).

Dublin: P Flynn; L Hickey, L Foley, C Kane; M Kissane, P Holden, N Fox; D Foley, S Behan; B McDonald (1-2), M Whelan, S Coen (0-3); G Davey, W Casey (0-1), D Ferguson (0-1).

◂◃◆▷▸

IT WAS A major come-down after all the success of the previous 12 months.

'It wasn't so much missing out on a fourth Leinster; it was not getting to the semi-final of the All-Ireland,' says Mickey.

'We wanted to kick on again.

'After matches, we would often go out to a dance. If it was summertime, no matter where we were coming back from, we would try and make it back to Dublin on time.

'I used to pal around with Paddy Holden and the two Foleys, Des and Lar. We would all go to a dance out in Red Island in Skerries.

'Even if we were playing in Belfast, we'd go to a dance. It was a classy way of doing it. Our wives and girlfriends would be all ready and dolled up. First we would go for a meal.

'Then we would head up to Skerries to dance the night away.

'Over the years, how we were treated by the County Board after games dramatically improved.

'When I first broke onto the county team, I used to walk home after playing matches in Croke Park.

'In 1963, I played in the All-Ireland final with a shirt that didn't even have a Dublin crest on it. But, slowly, things improved.

'The St Vincent's element on the County Board began to hold greater sway. Denis Mahony became chairman, and that changed how everything was run.

'We now live in different times, where players are more than adequately looked after. GAA life has changed for the better for our best footballers and hurlers. They deserve everything they now get.'

Parading before the 1963 All-Ireland final win over Galway (Mickey is fifth in line).

They never did get back to claim another All-Ireland title but Dublin of the 60s were still doing good work (here's Mickey before a charity outing, on the front left, with amongst others Kevin Heffernan, Luke Kelly, Niall Tóibín and Maureen Potter).

« CHAPTER 8 »

GETTING KNOCKED OUT in 1964 just showed the cut-and-thrust nature of championship football back then.

Back in those days, there was no second chance.

No backdoor.

When you were out… you were out.

'Everyone would prefer a second chance. It would have meant you got your bad day out of your system… you'd still be in with a chance.

'But a Leinster final loss to Meath, and that was it. It was all over for us. We had to wait until the following year.

'Of course, the backdoor did have its drawbacks for Dublin in more modern times.

'As I've already said, the team that Pat Gilroy and I inherited played their best football in the Leinster Championship – when there was a safety net in case the team tripped up. Once that safeguard was removed, however, the same Dublin team didn't last long in the All-Ireland series.

'When I played championship, you had to win. If you didn't win, you were gone. When it's knockout football, every game you go out to play is a final. And you had to treat it like that.

'You only find out what a team is made of when the chips are down.'

IN 2010, EVERYONE involved with the Dublin team knew they had to toughen up mentally. And that summer an opportunity presented itself.

Another Meath championship win over Dublin.

A bad day at the office all around sent Dublin hurtling for the qualifiers. This was an alien concept for the Dublin team, after winning five consecutive Leinster titles. But in hindsight, it might have been just the tonic.

Dublin were forced to play with their backs against the wall in the qualifiers. Wins over Tipperary, Armagh and Sligo got them back on track, and into an All-Ireland quarter-final.

Not only that, however.

It forced Dublin to play with no safety net for the entire summer.

THE OFF-SEASON IN 2009 was a fruitful one from Dublin's perspective. As explained, Pat Gilroy and Mickey Whelan met with every player individually to air out any issues, and plan for the coming year.

If this was a three-year project in their minds – and it was – they needed 2010 to be a year of real progress.

During those few winter months, Dublin identified Monaghan as a team against whom they would get real benefit from playing.

Monaghan were a tough, physical outfit. And Dublin figured that if they could front up and go toe-to-toe against them, they would be a match for anyone in the physical stakes.

The Dublin players were told before going out what they needed to do. It was not just one challenge game. Dublin played Monaghan several times over the course of a few months.

It suited Monaghan manager Seamus 'Banty' McEnaney too. He was looking at Dublin as a good football team and he wanted Dublin's scalp for his own team's confidence. They weren't necessarily looking for that physical battle, because that was already a strength of his team.

With the Monaghan players, Banty didn't have to worry about toughness.

'We needed our guys to come out, knock the stuffing out of the opposition, and play some good football,' explains Mickey.

'We needed to expose our lads to a team like Monaghan. Banty's brother, Pat McEnaney officiated the games. He was one of the top referees in the country.

There may or may not have been a word with him beforehand not to jump in too early, or be too whistle-happy!

'We wanted our lads to find themselves in a real war of attrition.

'It was played at the wrong time of the year too… in lashing rain and on winter nights. If our lads were up for a battle in those conditions, they would have the appetite to battle anywhere.'

◂◂◆▸▸

ALAN BROGAN

They were physical games. Pat and Mickey were very focused on the mental side of things. The physical side of things was easy to get right. That was easy for Mickey.

But I think the mental side of things was where we were lacking the previous few years. And Monaghan in the winter can be a tough place to go to.

That was the reasoning behind it.

They wanted to push us out of our comfort zone as much and as often as they possibly could… just to move the dial for people.

Those were tough, no-holes-barred games up there.

And I think both teams probably benefited from them. Players were going up there with a lot to prove. Monaghan were probably in the same boat.

It was an interesting time for sure!

◂◂◆▸▸

AFTER SEVERAL OF those matches, the Dublin management knew their lads were up for it. Then they started to concentrate on other aspects.

'We put an emphasis on everybody working hard when we weren't in possession. That included the corner-forwards. They were the first line of defence.

'If your man got the ball, you chased him. You made sure he didn't get it further out the field.

'Guys had to stick with their man and go that extra mile.

'And they had to show us in training that they were willing to do it. In the morning and in the evening. There was no love lost on the training field at times!

'We dropped some very good players during that period. And that gave them a choice. They could either put the head down, work hard and show us that they were happy to put in the hard yards that were required. Or they could lie down.

'One or the other.

'We had to build them up mentally. We had to front up physically and defensively. But we also had to use the ball smarter.

'They all improved in those areas.

'We also put men on individual programmes, for them to improve in areas we needed them to improve in.'

The training even brought Dublin out to Portugal.

As a reward for winning the Leinster Championship the team usually went on a holiday at the end of the year.

The management made sure that wives, partners and girlfriends were also invited. Gilroy and Whelan, from their own experience, were well aware who were the people in every home making the greatest sacrifices.

They all came, and had a great time.

But it was far from no work and all play.

During the day, the team had training sessions, and everyone had a meal together in the evening.

They bonded further as a team in Portugal.

ALL IN ALL, it was a hugely fruitful off-season.

Between the meetings with the players, the trip away, tough training sessions and battles with Monaghan, Dublin were well prepared for the upcoming National League.

And they hit the ground running.

The first assignment of the 2010 National League was massive. Dublin were up against Kerry… in Killarney. *Perfect.*

The stakes weren't as big as when they met the previous summer. But for Dublin, it was all about the next one. This was about laying down a marker, and delivering a statement. Not so much to the country at large, but to prove to themselves that they could beat them! *Beat Kerry!*

It also proved to the group as a whole that what they were doing was right.

The 6am training sessions were beginning to bear fruit.

'It's important to get to that stage, where you have full buy-in.

'After that Kerry win, every single player fully bought into what we were doing.

'It also proved to the group that we weren't as far off the pace as that 2009 All-Ireland Championship quarter-final defeat suggested. The 17-point hammering didn't do us justice.

'Beating Kerry in their own backyard just months after losing to them… that was a big thing for our gang.

'They had never beaten a Kerry team.

'It was massive for us. It's harder to beat a team in the championship, if you have no experience of getting one over on them in any contest before that.'

Wins over Derry, Mayo and Monaghan followed in that league campaign, which saw Dublin face Tyrone in the last game. Mickey Harte's side had been All-Ireland champions in 2008, and won Ulster the following year. They were still one of the top teams in the country, but were fighting to stay in Division 1.

Dublin were playing them away in Omagh. It was a must-win game for Tyrone. But Dublin went up there and delivered.

Bernard Brogan scored six points from play; his brother Alan bagged 1-1.

Dublin won 2-14 to 1-11.

Tyrone went *down* on the double.

'Wins like that massively boost belief.

'Another who got on the scoreboard that day was Niall Corkery from Kilmacud Crokes. What a player!

'He did a serious job for us in midfield, but after 2010 he opted out as he was moving to England with his partner. He was a massive loss.

'He came home for the All-Ireland final in 2011, and I talked to him at the post-match function. I felt really sorry for him, having missed out on the breakthrough by just one year. I knew what it is like missing out on All-Ireland medals because you had made the huge decision to emigrate.

'But at least I had one All-Ireland medal in my back pocket when I left the Dublin dressing-room and Ireland.

'Niall left 12 months too early.'

DUBLIN MISSED OUT, to Cork, on reaching the National League final on a head-to-head record, having finished level on points.

But it was a positive campaign. The team was improving all the time, and had delivered a few results that would really stand to them going forward. The championship opener against Wexford couldn't have started much worse, however. Dublin were flat.

'We were holding our wing-forwards quite deep, and they were using their two free half-backs to get by us.

'At half-time, they were well on top, leading 0-8 to 0-2.

'We needed to change something. We had a stern chat with the team that needed to be had – we also decided to go man-for-man after the break.

'We finally clicked into gear, pulling it level after 70 minutes. Extra-time was to be played, and we were the ones with all the momentum by that stage.

'We ended up winning 2-16 to 0-15. Bernard Brogan, who would go on to be named Footballer of the Year in 2010, was instrumental… scoring 2-4… all but one point came from play.'

BERNARD BROGAN WAS an obvious talent when he came into the Dublin camp. But the management team wanted him to play a bit more sensibly. Every time he got the ball, Brogan wanted to score. He used to shoot from virtually anywhere, but *anywhere* can be a wasteful shot.

Gilroy and Whelan wanted him to shoot from inside the scoring zones.

'Bernard has a great mentality, and he was happy to adapt. We also got him working harder for the team. And he was brilliant for us.

'After the first year with the group, it was a different team on the field. It was different training. It was all with the ball. And Bernard slotted into the new system, pulling in the same direction as everyone else.

'He had the ability and he had the pace. It was all about harnessing that in the best way possible for the team as a whole.'

ALAN BROGAN

Pat would have looked after a lot of the forward play and how we approached the game when we had the ball. But Mickey was very much involved with what we did when we didn't have possession.

I think for a period of time, Mickey wasn't worried about our attack.

He trusted we knew what we were doing when we had the ball! But it was the other side of it that he really wanted to work on with us.

For two years, he was onto the likes of myself and Bernard, who might not have had a reputation for working really hard off the ball, and he was at us relentlessly for a couple of years to try and improve that. A huge focus of his first couple of years was getting a higher workrate out of the forwards that were on the field.

◄◄◆▶▶

AT HALF-TIME in that Wexford match, Dublin were booed off the pitch by some supporters. They weren't happy.

One newspaper report observed: *As the Dublin players left the field with a 0-8 to 0-2 deficit at the interval, they were jeered by their own supporters. Derision on the Hill grew louder when Mattie Forde stretched Wexford's lead, and the Dubs shot a succession of wides, some of them well off the mark.*

They weren't booing in the second-half, that's for sure.

'When I was manager in the 90s, I saw how it could turn nasty. In those intervening years, I would be walking out of Croke Park and down Clonliffe Road after Dublin exited the championship.

'Thousands of people there might not be turning up at a GAA game again until the following summer.

'County championship and National League games would rarely if ever fill Parnell Park. You would never get more than a few thousand at club games in Dublin, and most of the National League games down through those years were held in Donnycarney.

'So, if all the real followers were at those matches, the other 50,000 or whatever who turn up on the big days in the summer must be just going for the day out.

'But that day against Wexford showed to us that the team's mental resolve was growing. They were improving.

'I'm not sure if the Dublin team of the previous year, or before that again, would have recovered from a six-point deficit at half-time, having only scored two points.

'That cemented some players' positions, as we knew they had what it takes to dig deep when the going got tougher.

'Against Meath the next day, however, we were carved open at the back.

'They tore us apart, and got in for goals. They were killing us at midfield and then cutting right through us.'

◄◄◆▷►

2010 LEINSTER SFC SEMI-FINAL
MEATH 5-9 DUBLIN 0-13

Meath put an end to nine barren years by blitzing champions Dublin in the Leinster football semi-final. An electrifying exhibition of goal finishing was the main charge that surged through the winners' display and completely stunned the favourites.

If Dublin had to conduct extensive debugging of their defensive programme two weeks previously against Wexford, yesterday the whole system crashed, leaving Meath's sharp forward lines free to cut them apart.

The most striking thing was how little composure the champions showed, as the match lurched against them at the end of the third quarter. There was neither the belief amongst the more senior players nor the experience amongst their younger teammates to plot an escape route.

◄◄◆▷►

A LOT WAS said after that defeat.

There was a great deal to be ironed out, and it was a tough time. It showed Dublin were far from the finished article.

However, the big defeat gave the management team the freedom to rectify some shortcomings. They made a few personnel switches, and dropped some players. That date remains the last time that Dublin have lost a Leinster Championship match.

'It highlighted that work still needed to be done. We had a couple of get-togethers to air it out. The only blessing was perhaps it was a Leinster semi-final, rather than a final. If we were facing into a crunch match the following weekend, we might have been in trouble. We would have been up against a team who had built up momentum in the qualifiers.

'We were drawn against Tipperary in the backdoor, and had two weeks to prepare. The fortnight break between the two games was valuable, as we got them into the right headspace. A post-mortem is needed after a defeat like that.

'I remember Paul Casey being particularly excellent in the group around that time. He was a great bit of stuff. While he might not have been starting, and often captained the B team in training matches, his enthusiasm and leadership rubbed off on other players.

'Those A vs B matches were fiercely contested and massively competitive. We would let them go hell-for-leather... then pull them out for running, before resuming the match.

'Paul might not have been making the first 15, but was still giving it everything and helping to drive the whole thing on.

'That qualifier run helped us to build momentum.'

It was win or bust. There was no longer the insurance of a second bite at the cherry. This was the last chance saloon.

Dublin didn't set the world alight against Tipp, but did enough to win 1-21 to 1-13. They faced a step-up against Armagh the following week.

◄ ◄◆▸ ▸

2010 ALL-IRELAND SFC QUALIFIER
DUBLIN 0-14 ARMAGH 0-11

A Bernard Brogan-inspired Dublin passed another test of their Championship mettle as they battled past Armagh.

Dublin's defence certainly looked more composed than it has done this summer, but too much hand-passing and not enough direct football from the Orchard men played into the winners' hands, allowing them to keep their structure throughout.

Dublin's greater mobility and the addition of some power off the bench – Darren Magee and Eamon Fennell saw second-half action – gave them a deserved win in the end. But their over-reliance on Bernard Brogan for scores will cause concern.

Armagh, the NFL Division 2 champions, could not stop the St Oliver Plunkett's/ Eoghan Ruadh clubman from wielding his influence on proceedings. When a better side does, the question is does Pat Gilroy have a plan B?

That answer is for another day.

◄ ◄◆▸ ▸

DUBLIN THEN BEAT Louth, 2-14 to 0-13.

Louth, a team Mickey Whelan managed himself in the 80s, had been robbed the previous weekend in the Leinster Championship final. They were always going to find it tough, after a controversial Meath goal had denied them their first provincial title since 1957. Dublin showed they were far from reliant on Bernard Brogan that day, with Eoghan O'Gara scoring 2-1 at full-forward. After three consecutive wins, they found themselves back in an All-Ireland quarter-final. But in contrast to other years, they had not come through the direct route.

'Was it a blessing in disguise that we were beaten in Leinster that year? I wouldn't say yes. You want to win as many championship medals as you can. But that loss to Meath did expose us to a few different experiences that summer, and we were well prepared coming into the last eight.

'Standing in our way was Tyrone, who had won the Ulster title. After we had relegated them a few months previously, we knew we had what it took to beat them again in the championship.

'It was a huge win. To beat one of the country's top teams in an All-Ireland quarter-final was something Dublin had been crying out for. Bernard Brogan scored nine points, four of which came from play... and he didn't kick a wide! Eoghan O'Gara's goal in the 65th minute put us three points up and sent us on our way.'

◄◄◆▷►

2010 ALL-IRELAND SFC QUARTER-FINAL
DUBLIN 1-15 TYRONE 0-13

Pat Gilroy sifted through the ashes of last year's horror show against Kerry and came to the conclusion that for all the county's provincial dominance, Dublin needed to go back to the drawing board if they were going to compete with the best teams.

His painstakingly devised defence-orientated system, emphasising work rate, cover and fast-breaking counter-attack, trialled well during the league but had fallen apart at the onset of the championship. The voyage through the qualifiers was generally seen as holding the promise of only partial redemption. Gilroy himself admitted afterwards that beating a top-three county hadn't formed part of the management's expectations for this season. A work in progress that would be competitive was the measured hope.

Dublin's outsider status released the intense and unreasonable pressure under which they had laboured against Kerry and Tyrone in the previous two years.

◄ ◄ ◆ ▷ ►

'I KNEW THAT we had the beating of Tyrone, after relegating them earlier in that league. That quarter-final victory was a great win, particularly given that we had been thrashed by Meath in Leinster.

'It showed the progress we had made in the space of the 18 months we had been with the panel. We had not won the Leinster Championship in 2010, but it was far more important to get to an All-Ireland semi-final, and still be in the hunt for the Sam Maguire Cup.'

Unfortunately, the season came to a shuddering halt against Cork in the semi-final. It was a game Dublin dominated, and they led for the majority of the contest. However, it got away from them in the end. Eoghan O'Gara was causing havoc at full-forward, and the Cork backs were struggling to deal with him.

'We took him off in the last 10 minutes, and that was a mistake.

'He could have kept going all day.

'Neither did we get the breaks. In the 53rd minute, Cork were awarded a sideline after the ball had clearly gone out off one of their own men. A small thing, maybe. But they let the ball in long and won a penalty. Donncha O'Connor put the ball in the net… the goal changed the game.

'They beat us by a point.'

◄ ◄ ◆ ▷ ►

2010 ALL-IRELAND SFC SEMI-FINAL
CORK 1-15 DUBLIN 1-14

It was a game Cork should never have won. For 55 minutes Pat Gilroy's young Dublin side controlled a fascinating semi-final at Croke Park. They played with a rabid intensity that never dropped, not for one moment, and stifled and frustrated Cork to the point where Conor Counihan's men looked a pale shadow of the team that has become one of the dominant forces of the modern game.

Cork attacked and attacked and kept coming up empty, as Dublin showed an unrestrained zeal and desire to go about their defensive duties. They stripped Cork of the ball time after time and closed down the space so that the Rebels looked like they were entangled in poison ivy every time they crossed into the Dublin half.

However, Dublin's plan had a flaw and it was exposed as the game entered the final quarter. The intensity remained constant but the concentration levels dropped in the closing stages and their discipline suffered as a result.

◄◄◆►►

2010 WAS ONE that got away.

Dublin thought they should have won that All-Ireland title. It led to a winter of regret.

Granted, it was a three-year project. And Dublin were a better team in 2011 than they were in 2010. But nonetheless, they felt they were there or thereabout in year two.

'We could have beaten Cork in that semi-final, and they went on to win the All-Ireland.

'Fine margins.

'But we were moving in the right direction. We were becoming more solid in defence, and playing together as a team.

'That was also the year that Stephen Cluxton started taking our long-range frees. It was a decision we made as a management.

'We had no consistency in free-takers up to that point, and it's something we needed to nail down. Mossy Quinn and Conal Keaney were among those taking them, but sometimes they weren't starting.

'Stephen was reliable. He was strong mentally.

'And boy did he do a job for us.

'He's a lovely guy. Even during the coronavirus lockdown over the last year, at the time of writing this book, he rang me twice to make sure I was doing okay... if I needed shopping done, or anything else?

'That's a measure of the man.

'A great human being.'

Dublin were sent crashing out of Leinster in 2010 when Meath fired five goals past them (above), but the team continued to grow through the summer even though Pat Gilroy (right) had another disappointing day when Conor Counihan's Cork beat them in the All-Ireland semi-final.

The players were adapting fast to what was required of them if they were to be the best team in the country, and nobody exemplified that more than Bernard Brogan who learned to match his scoring skills with a massive work ethic.

« CHAPTER 9 »

CLANNA GAEL HAD been knocking on the door of a county championship for several years throughout the 60s. They reached Dublin SFC finals in 1962 and '63, but were unable to clear the final hurdle. Bar the odd interjection from UCD, St Vincent's continued to rule the roost in those years.

The 1962 final was Kevin Heffernan's last match before retirement, and Vincent's edged it 3-13 to 3-8. Clanna Gael tore into a 2-1 to 0-1 lead early on but ultimately fell short. They would have to wait for a few more years, though they had a strong team in those years. Paddy Holden and Mickey were on the Dublin team and had won Cú Chulainn Awards throughout the decade. Gerry Davey, Christy Kane, Aidan Donnelly and Tony Gilleen all played for Dublin during that period. Mick Byrne, who later went on to become physio for the Republic of Ireland soccer team, was on the side too, and was a gifted gaelic footballer.

Clanna Gael also had a few country men. Thady O'Donoghue, father of Paddy who was a selector alongside Mickey under Pat Gilroy in 2011, was also on the side. Losing those county finals was shattering. They were massive occasions, with anything up to 30,000 supporters in Croke Park.

They then won the league in 1967, which was a big deal with St Vincent's being so strong around then.

◄◄◆►►

CLANNA GAEL
MONTHLY CLUB NEWSLETTER
1967

Since these notes last appeared, the one Senior League match we did play was in Croke Park vs St Vincent's. This was a match we were given little chance of winning; indeed the Dublin County Board assumed we would be defeated and arranged to finish the league with a top-four play-off. The Board Officials, however, received a rude shock, for we defeated the county champions by a point in a most exciting game.

We should have won by a greater score but the forward weakness shown throughout 1967 was very much in evidence. Our backs, however, were magnificent. Christy Kane made the journey from Scotland to play full-back and right well did he acquit himself. Jim McGill and John McDermott were others to play above themselves in our defence.

The match will, however, be remembered as Mickey Whelan's match. He gave a power-packed display at midfield and scored all but one point of our winning total. His goal from a 14-yard free was the result of one of the hardest ground shots ever seen in Croke Park. The ball hit the back of the net before the Vincent's backs realised it had been kicked.

This was truly your greatest hour in Clanna Gael, Mickey.

◄ ◄ ◆ ► ►

AHEAD OF THE 1968 season, Ted Coolin, who was the chairman of Clanna Gael at the time, asked Mickey to coach the team.

'But Ted. I'm not finished yet… I want to play!' Mickey retorted.

'No, of course you'll still be playing, Mickey. But we want you to train them as well as play!'

Mickey Whelan was only turning 29 that year, so he still had plenty to offer on the field of play. But after being asked to manage the side at the same time, he was happy to go along with that. The club had not won the county title in 20 years – a drought they badly wanted to end.

It was a task Mickey may not have had the confidence to undertake a few years beforehand. But winning an All-Ireland medal with Dublin and playing for Leinster's Railway Cup side helped to build his self-belief.

He would design all the training sessions, and then take part in them too.

With the added responsibility of being manager and coach, Mickey did not want to be captain of the side too. He decided to appoint Maurice 'Mossie' O'Driscoll, a Kerry man from Valentia, to the role.

It was not Mickey's first time coaching. He was doing bits here and there. But it was certainly his biggest gig up to that point.

It was a tricky balancing act, but one he relished.

Clanna Gael reached the county final that year, overcoming Na Fianna in a hard fought match at the penultimate stage. As luck would have it, St Vincent's had already been eliminated.

But it was by no means a foregone conclusion.

Scoil Uí Chonaill were their opponents in the decider at Croke Park.

It was a game, however, that Clanna Gael easily won, 1-8 to 0-5.

◂◂◆▷▸

1968 DUBLIN SFC FINAL
CLANNA GAEL 1-8 SCOIL UÍ CHONAILL 0-5

Clanna Gael won the Dublin senior football title at Croke Park yesterday for one reason and one reason only – they had Mickey Whelan.

Not only did Whelan notch seven of his team's nine scores, he also starred at midfield and in defence. He also placed Victor Black in the fourth minute for the only goal of the match from a close free.

Neither team ever played the combined football of which they are capable, but Whelan when in possession – and he played more of the ball than any man afield – produced constructive, brainy football, and almost single-handedly carried his club to the title that had eluded them for more than 20 years.

Scoil Uí Chonaill were particularly unsettled in the opening minutes and Clann's early goal looked the prelude to a convincing victory, but there was nothing at all between them through the rest of a madly scrambling first-half that yielded three points from play and three from frees to leave Clans still that goal ahead, 1-3 to 0-3 at half-time.

Whelan, who won the only major honour that had so far eluded him, lined out at midfield instead of his scheduled half-forward post, and received assistance from defenders Tom Walsh, Christy Kane, Paddy Holden and Gerry Davey.

Scorers: Clanna Gael – M Whelan (0-7), V Black (1-0), J Taylor (0-1); Scoil Ui Chonaill – S O'Donoghue (0-5).

◄◄◆►►

WINNING THAT COUNTY title was special.

Mickey had been lucky enough to win it all with Dublin – National League, Leinster and All-Ireland titles. He had won a Railway Cup medal with Leinster. But club glory had eluded him up to that point.

It was the final piece of the jigsaw.

It would have been a huge regret had he moved to America without winning a county title with Clanna Gael.

◄◄◆►►

MICK BYRNE

Mickey was an outstanding player. He won all the honours in the game, including Railway Cup titles, and I would put him in the same mould as Kevin Keegan and Georgie Best in terms of quality, albeit in a different sport.

He would have made it as a soccer player as well.

He got an offer from Drumcondra but wanted to keep playing football. He was a wonderful reader of gaelic football.

In 1968, he was our top player, trainer... the lot. He had all the moves worked out... he had pace, a good dummy and he was a great passer of the ball.

◄◄◆►►

CLANNA GAEL WAS not Mickey Whelan's local club growing up. Reared in Cabra West, St Finbarr's and a few other clubs were closer.

But Mossy O'Connor, a teacher in St Peter's National School, brought a few of the young lads including Mickey down to Ringsend to play. Mossy never taught Mickey in school, but Paddy Woods must have told him that he was a good player.

Mr Woods pulled Mickey aside one day and said that Mr O'Connor wanted a word with him. Mickey thought he was in trouble, perhaps he had done something wrong in the schoolyard!

'Mickey, Mr Woods tells me that you're a good player. Would you be interested in coming out and playing gaelic football with the school team?' Mr O'Connor asked.

Mickey had never played gaelic football before. He had played lots of soccer on the streets and after school with Mr Woods, while he played a lot of hurling on the street where he lived. Mickey also played hurling in the street leagues. Mr Woods assured Mickey that he had all the transferable skills required.

Mickey agreed to give gaelic football a try.

Mr O'Connor and Mr Woods were great role models and brilliant schoolteachers.

They were great at overseeing matches and helping young lads to improve. Mr O Connor brought them up to the Phoenix Park every day after school. He would have two teams picked, and the boys would play their hearts out until Mr. O'Connor called time at six o clock by his watch.

However, if there was something Mr O'Connor could help with, he would not pause the whole game to deliver a message. When the ball was down the other end of the pitch, he would walk over and simply say, 'Hey Mickey, did you see Johnny Bogan there?'

'No. I was looking for Paddy Holden!'

He would then suggest, 'You've plenty of time on the ball. Don't be afraid to look around and see if there are any other options'.

There was no stopping the game.

When the game was down the other end, he'd slip in… offer advice, and back out. Nobody was embarrassed.

'They were brilliant at enabling us to learn,' Mickey remembers.

'We could all learn from that philosophy.'

'GOOD COACHES DON'T teach… they facilitate the learning of skills.

'They encourage and facilitate.

'Looking back, Paddy Woods and Mossy O'Connor were brilliant teachers and excellent enablers facilitating us.

'We had a brilliant school team at that time. We got to the cup final against Scoil Mhuire, who were largely a St Vincent's team.

'From the teams that played that day, Des Foley, Noel Fox, Paddy Holden and myself went on to win All-Ireland medals in 1963.

◄◄◆►►

1952 SWEET AFTON CUP
(DIVISION 1 FINAL)

Players from St Peter's Boys National School, Phibsboro have gone on to hit the headlines in inter-county competitions. Mickey Whelan and Paddy Holden helped Dublin to their All-Ireland Senior Football Championship final win in 1963. Both also played with Leinster and won Railway Cup medals as well, and they were in the Clanna Gael team that won the Dublin Senior Football Championship in 1968.

Holden and Whelan were both in a school team that lost the Sweet Afton Cup final by a last minute point to Marino. The Marino team included Des Foley and Noel Fox, who both also created big impressions on the inter-county front, and that Sweet Afton Cup team is rated among one of the best St Peter's teams of all time.

◄◄◆►►

EVEN OUTSIDE OF 'structured' sport, it was all well-organised playing on the roads and the parks when Mickey Whelan grew up.

They often used to play alongside the Royal Canal. And some of the older boys, when they got thirsty during a match, would go over to the canal and drink out of it!

Mickey thought that odd.

'I often saw dead pups floating by it in bags... floating down the canal. If people had dogs and didn't want the pups, they would drown them and throw them in the canal. Awful stuff.

'And our guys were drinking that water!'

Mickey remembers raising his concerns.

'No, Mickey!' they told him. 'Look at the cowboys! They always say... once it's running water, you can drink it!'

He too had seen pictures of cowboys where they would get off their horses to have a drink out of a river.

'We thought we were doing the same thing. Crazy stuff, looking back!

'The funny thing is, as a young lad on school holidays I swam a lot in the canal and I am sure I swallowed the odd gulp of water while swimming or messing with my pals, and I am still around. Thankfully, I have never gotten seriously ill. I occasionally wonder did it affect my immune system in any way.

'It's said that whatever doesn't kill you makes you stronger.

'Not that I would advise anybody to do it!'

PLAYING WITH CLANNA Gael in Ringsend meant there was a commute involved. It was not the local club, so Mickey used to have to get the bus.

On the days they had training or a match, his mother would give him his bus fare.

'I would be waiting by the roundabout for the bus, and sometimes older boys would be playing pitch-and-toss there.

'On one occasion, I lost my bus fare before the bus even arrived. There was no way I would be going back to my mother to tell her that I had lost it gambling!! At sixteen years of age!

'She would have murdered me!

'So, on that occasion, I had to grab the plastic bag with my knicks, boots and stockings… and I ran, jogged, and walked from Cabra West down to Ringsend.

'Down the North Circular Road…

'All the way through onto the quays…

'And down then to Ringsend. It must have been five miles!

'And I then played a match. I don't recall ever being too wrecked, but that run must have taken it out of me!'

The run to Ringsend was a far more attractive prospect than returning home to inform his mother he had lost the money playing pitch-and-toss!

After matches, Ted Cooling would give the boys a lift halfway home.

He lived in Raheny, so he dropped the three Cabra West guys – Paddy Holden, Johnny Bogan and Mickey – off at the bottom of the North Circular Road.

MICKEY PLAYED GAELIC football with Clanna Gael, and hurling with Fontenoys. The two clubs have since amalgamated.

They played in Ringsend Park, which used to be known as 'Iodine Park'. This was because at that time, there were stones, bits of glass and shards of metal from the nearby factories on the pitch. It was called 'Iodine Park' because any time somebody fell and scratched themselves, the iodine needed to be taken out and rubbed on the wound!

There was a good underage team in Clanna Gael, and they often won the southside tournaments. That then pitted them against St Vincent's, who would be too strong, and won almost everything at underage.

'I am often asked how, since I was living in Cabra West, that I came to play for Clanna Gael and Fontenoys. The simple answer is that after my first year playing for the school, Mr O'Connor asked me would I consider joining Clanna Gael and, if I was interested, I should discuss it with my parents. Four of us got permission from our parents – and the late Johnny Bogan, Matthew Walsh, Paddy Holden and myself.

'Unfortunately, Matthew died in his early twenties from an illness, and Johnny Bogan, who was Best Man at my wedding, and an excellent hurler and footballer, in addition to being a thorough gentleman, also died too young. But Paddy, Johnny and myself spent many enjoyable years playing with Clanna Gael and Fontenoys. The Fletcher brothers kept hurling alive in Fontenoys and were very important in the amalgamation process with Clanna Gael.'

During his last two years in primary school, Mickey represented the Dublin schools' teams. A Dublin selection faced a Belfast team in football and hurling each alternative year, in Belfast one year and in Dublin the next.

'I played midfield on the hurling team in Belfast, a game which we won. I remember being awarded a medal for it... my first time ever winning one, which was a big deal for me at the time.

'I was beaming with pride bringing it home to show it to my parents. I played on the winning football team in Croke Park the following year as well.

'Those years in Clanna Gael were a great experience, and a great upbringing. I played every type of sport in school. I even boxed for a brief while. When I was in primary school, I competed in athletics. I was a good high jumper. We used to practice it in the playground, jumping over sticks. I ended up competing in the

Dublin Primary Schools' competition in Croke Park. I jumped four foot, seven inches at around the age of 14. On the same day, I ran the second leg of the relay which we won.

'I came second in the hurdles competition, also a discipline which I had never tried up to that day. I remember the race... I just ran... flicked a leg up over the obstacle... and RAN! I lost pace while going over the hurdles, but I would make up the lost ground by sprinting in between.

'I made sure to finish strong... there was a long run-in to the finish line.

'The array of sports was always important. In hindsight, they all probably helped me to develop as an athlete.'

AFTER TWO YEARS in the Technical School, he started a five-year apprenticeship at the age of 16. His mother always wanted Mickey to go to college. But his father was encouraging him to go for the apprenticeship.

He remembers his father sitting the two of them down one day, when they were weighing up the decision.

'Listen Colleen, do you want young Michael to emigrate... do you?' he asked her.

'No. Of course not... not at all.'

'Well, all the graduates who are coming out of universities with degrees... they are all emigrating because there is no work for people with those kinds of skills here in Ireland. If you want to keep Michael here in Ireland, an apprenticeship is the solution. They can never get enough apprentices.'

And that was that. Mickey's mother did not want him to move abroad. And Mickey did not want to go away either.

'MY PARENTS WERE great. My father Frank Whelan was a native of Phibsboro. He was a boiler-maker by trade and, as I've said, he worked on the building of power stations around the country.

'His father was from Wexford, and his mother was a Dublin woman.

'When he was in the army, along with his twin brother Matt, they both competed in boxing tournaments.

'The army championship was fought on the one night. If you won your fight, you waited until the next one. You kept going until you were defeated.

'As it turned out, both twins were middleweights and reached the final. But their father, my grandfather, would not let them fight one another. He pulled them aside, and flipped a coin instead. My father won the coin toss, and was told he was the winner.

'I never saw any medals around the house for boxing but I saw one gold medal and a couple of silver runner-up medals on a gold chain for soccer. One day, I asked him what he got for winning the army championship. He said he was given a free meal in the posh canteen, the Officers Mess. That was a big deal, he told me.

'They both spent about a year in the army. Matt never married. He ended up living with my parents in later years after I had moved out.

'The military background clearly rubbed off on the pair. My father always made sure to shine his boots, and he dressed well. Another value that was important to him was never lying.

'No matter what, you stood up and told the truth.

'Those traits were embedded in me from a young age.

'MY MOTHER COLLEEN Drumm, was born in the Rotunda Hospital and lived in Hardwicke Street. She had four brothers and one sister.

'At Christmas time there would always be a party and singsong in our house on New Year's Eve. There would always be the occasional bit of leg pulling involved. On one occasion I heard my uncle Benny respond to my uncle Tom, saying, "I did time for you! I went to jail for you… remember that", and there was great laughter.

'I was shocked. An uncle in jail… and everyone laughing. I could not wait to question my mam when all had left.

'My mam said he was in jail, but stressed that he didn't do anything wrong! His brother Tom was a soldier, she explained, and ended up on the losing side. He was arrested and he was imprisoned overseas, in Frongoch prison in Wales.'

The story goes that one time the family home was raided. The front door was burst down with guns, by those looking for Thomas Drumm.

Mickey's grandfather immediately piped up.

'THERE HE IS!' and he pointed at Benny!

Benny was protesting. 'It's not me! It's not me!'

'Don't mind him!' Mickey's grandfather told them. 'Take him!'

Tom was in bed in the room next door. There were wooden boxes alongside him, all filled with arms.

'Had they knocked into that room, Tom would have been in serious trouble and may even have died attempting to escape,' continues Mickey.

'So my grandfather fingered out Benny instead.

'They took Benny, thinking they had captured Thomas Drumm.

'He was in prison for about seven or eight days before my grandfather went down with Benny's mother to the place. "Listen!" he told them. "You are looking for that other fella! You took this fella... he's the wrong man!"

'They had to go through the processes and stuff to verify that this in fact was not Tom. He was eventually let go. But any time down through the years that they were having a bit of craic when all the family was gathered, Benny was quick to remind Tom that he spent time in captivity on his behalf!

'Tom subsequently did end up getting arrested at some point, and was brought to prison. He got out eventually, and was quite ill upon his release. His chest was very poor because of the conditions in the prison.

'He was a lovely man!'

'I HAVE FOUR siblings, and we're all still alive.

'I am the eldest. My three sisters are Frances, Ann and Joan.

'Frances and Ann played camogie for Naomh Aoife. Frances won two Dublin championship medals and one league medal with the club, and she also won two All-Ireland medals with Dublin. Ann won one championship and one league medal with Naomh Aoife. As I've already said, Joan, my youngest sister, preferred tennis and rounders.

'Matthew was the youngest member of the family, and soccer became his passion. He played League of Ireland for three years; one year with St Patrick's Athletic and two with Shamrock Rovers. Matthew was also asked to sign with Bohemians.

'Bohs wanted him to play in a midweek game, but Matthew informed them he had booked and paid for a trip to a racecourse in England. He told them he'd be available the following week, but naturally they told him to play in the midweek game or they wouldn't sign him. He went to the races, and that was the end of his professional football career.

'I was in the U.S. at the time, and I regret not being there for him because I think I could have resolved the problem. He continued to play at the next level down and enjoyed his football career for many more years.

'It was certainly a sporting house growing up!

'That came from my mother and father. My mother was a very good Irish dancer, winning many Feiseanna medals as a child and a young woman, while my dad was a talented soccer player. He broke his leg in a bad tackle at 18 years of age.

When his leg was healed and he was almost ready to play again, he tripped and fell down the stairs at home. The leg broke a second time, and that ended my dad's football career. The surgeon warned him that if the leg was fractured a third time, it might have to be amputated.'

'WHEN I LEFT the Technical School, I started an apprenticeship as a fitter and turner, learning to repair machinery and engines and maintain the trucks on the road for the company that employed me. I also played soccer for the company on Saturdays in a factory league from the age of 17 alongside and against 20- and 30-year-old men.

'I had great experiences during my apprenticeship.

'It all built my confidence in a lot of ways. I found skills that would benefit me throughout my life.

' I was apprenticed to a man called Richard Morgan. I learned so much from him, and I played alongside him on the factory league team. At the end of each day when we were wrapping up, it was my duty to collect all the tools, and they had to be cleaned and placed back in the exact order as they were when opened in the morning. He wanted every tool to go back in the same spot.

'After working under him for so long, I ended up like that.

'Throughout my life, everything has to be in order! No shortcuts.

'And that applies across the board. If you take shortcuts in anything, you will likely have to end up doing the business all over again. Do things right the first time around. My apprenticeship and home gave me that philosophy.'

IT IS A regret of his that he never won another All-Ireland title with Dublin.

Not that it keeps Mickey awake at night. He was still happy with his lot. The one Celtic Cross from 1963 is something of which he remains forever proud.

It did not quite happen for Dublin for the remainder of the 60s.

In 1965, they regained the Leinster Championship title. By this stage, Mickey was no longer on free-taking duty. A young buck by the name of Jimmy Keaveney had broken into the team, and was not too bad on placed balls.

◄◄◆►►

1965 LEINSTER SFC QUARTER-FINAL
DUBLIN 2-11 WEXFORD 0-7

Perhaps the most encouraging feature of the game from a Dublin viewpoint was the accurate long-range shooting of the forwards. Whelan, who had his most successful outing for quite some time at centre half-forward, fired over three excellent points while Keaveney and Davey were others to take their chances in opportunist style.

◄◄◆►►

DUBLIN COMFORTABLY ACCOUNTED for Kildare in Tullamore three weeks later, 1-11 to 0-5, to qualify for the final.

Longford provided the opposition at Croke Park in the Leinster final. Jimmy Keaveney, Des Foley and Brian McDonald all found the net in a 3-6 to 0-9 victory. It was the fourth Leinster title of Mickey's career in the space of seven seasons.

Little did he know then it would prove to be his last with Dublin.

Not that he was thinking too far ahead. Kerry provided the opposition in the All-Ireland semi-final, a team he had never beaten in the championship.

Unfortunately, it was not to be. Kerry ran out 4-8 to 2-6 winners. A second All-Ireland medal eluded him that year, and that was as close as he came.

BUT 1965 WAS a memorable year for a variety of other reasons away from the football field. Irene and Mickey married that year. They married in Finglas, with the function afterwards at the Marine Hotel in Howth. They then moved into their home in Sutton Park. Their first son Cormac was born the following year.

Shane followed in 1968. They then had three daughters Michelle, Colleen and Emma over the following 10 years.

THROUGHOUT THE LATE-60s, Dublin receded from the main stage in gaelic football. The straight knockout format was a cruel one. One defeat and the summer was over. They suffered early exits at the hands of Kildare, Westmeath and Longford in 1966, '67 and '68 respectively.

The Leinster Championship was hugely competitive at the time. There were no games to be taken for granted. And Dublin learned that the hard way. They failed to get out of the province after 1965 for the rest of the decade.

Mickey captained the team in 1969, off the back of Clanna Gael's county final win the year beforehand. They accounted for Laois in the Leinster quarter-final, 3-7 to 1-5, before taking on Kildare in the semi-final in Carlow.

◄ ◄ ◆ ► ►

1969 LEINSTER SFC SEMI-FINAL
KILDARE 0-18 DUBLIN 0-7

The long football adolescence of Kildare is nearly over, if one is to judge by yesterday's upheaval of form at Dr Cullen Park, Carlow where Dublin, after looking like probable winners at half-time, were crushed by an 11-point margin in the Leinster semi-final.

It is, of course a possibility that Kildare's performance may have been exaggerated by as feeble a Dublin team as has worn the sky blue jersey.

Kildare's Peter Archibald must now surely rank high in the list of wing-half backs in the game. Yesterday, Archibald blotted out no less a man than Mickey Whelan.

◄ ◄ ◆ ► ►

AFTER THE HIGHS in the first half of the decade, the 60s petered out from a Dublin perspective.

Nobody could have guessed at that point that one of the county's most successful ever periods was just around the corner. Mickey Whelan didn't realise either, walking out of Dr Cullen Park that day, that he had played his final ever match in a Dublin jersey.

The winning St Peter's National School team from 1952/53 (Mickey is fourth from left in the front, with his life-long teammate Paddy Holden second from the left).

The Clanna Gael team finally clinched the Dublin senior football championship in 1968.

« CHAPTER 10 »

IN 1964, DUBLIN didn't manage to hold onto the Sam Maguire Cup. They did however enjoy the consolation of heading to New York, having won the National League 'Home' final.

They played against the Exiles in the Big Apple in the final proper.

They were also over there to enjoy themselves. John 'Kerry' O'Donnell, the famous Irish businessman in New York, whom Mickey Whelan would come to know quite well in later years, hosted the team.

The day before the match, he brought them on a walking tour all around the city in intense heat.

It was a long day, and the 'tour' carried on into the evening until about 11pm. By the time it came to an end that night, Dublin were wrecked!

John 'Kerry' was Mr New York GAA.

He had the lease on Gaelic Park.

But did he know full well what he was doing that day, tiring Dublin out before the match? In the game itself, Dublin also found it hard enough to get many decisions from the referee.

The four umpires were barmen, whom Mickey would also get to know at a later point in his life. Dublin fell just short.

◄◄◆►►

1964 NFL FINAL
NEW YORK 2-12 DUBLIN 1-13

New York won the National Football League title for the second time when in a dramatic finish at Gaelic Park yesterday, they held off a tremendous Dublin fight-back to win by 2-12 to 1-13 in a temperature of over 80 degrees. The game built up to a spectacular climax as Dublin, 0-6 down going into the last quarter, staked everything on a whirlwind finish.

Mickey Whelan showed a return to his best form at centre half-forward... with only one minute, four seconds left on the clock, it seemed certain that the Metropolitans would salvage a draw when they were awarded a 14-yard free straight in front of the posts. But John Timmons, so often the saviour of the team, failed with the crucial kick and the Americans swept upfield through a spread-eagled Dublin defence to claim the win with a point from Pat Cummins with virtually the last kick of the game.

◄◄◆►►

DUBLIN STAYED AROUND for another week, and played New York again a week later in a challenge game. It was a match they won.

'However, what I remember most about that second game was just before the throw-in, I met Bobby Kennedy. President John F Kennedy was shot and killed 11 months previously. But his brother Robert, or 'Bobby', was quickly making waves himself on the political scene. RFK was running to be in the U.S. Senate, and arrived at Gaelic Park for the match.

'I was captaining the team, and he came over for a quick chat with the two captains before the throw-in.

'He mentioned how he was Irish, and how his ancestors had come over to America. I was concentrating on the match, but was amazed to see him there.'

Bobby Kennedy himself was assassinated, in 1968, continuing the tragic tale of the Kennedy family.

◄◄◆►►

'IT WAS NO easy decision to move to America in 1969. I was leaving a life behind. I was leaving my friends, family and inter-county GAA behind. I even had to go over initially without Irene and our kids.

'Irene was to follow me out.

'After we had married in 1965, we had bought our family home in Sutton Park. It was a big financial stretch, but Kevin Heffernan advised me to go for it.

'He told me that the longer I left it, the more the house prices would increase.'

'Listen Mickey, it's a fine house,' he said. 'You can't afford it now. But in six years' time or so, the way money's value deteriorates, you will be well able to pay your mortgage and you'll have a house.

'If you wait to try and save to get to that, you won't be able to afford it then. The house will have gone up in value.'

Mickey remembers the conversation as one of the best pieces of advice he received at that time in his life.

'I was working my way up the ranks from my apprenticeship in Finglas.

'I then joined Roadstone. It was a good place to work, and I was doing a good job and there was variety. But in that industry, people could get laid off. There was no real job security at that time. And there were lots of places shutting down.

'I was very aware that I needed to provide for, and protect, my family.

'By this stage I also realised I wanted to become a teacher.'

MOVING TO AMERICA wasn't Mickey's first port of call.

He wanted to become a teacher, and went into Trinity College to investigate the possibility of studying there. The person he met from Trinity knew Mickey from gaelic football, but told him that it was unlikely he would get a place.

Mickey consulted with several people, but ultimately he decided that moving to America was the best option he had in finally building a new career.

'We decided I would move out on my own first and get set up, before Irene would follow me out with the kids.

'It was awful being apart.

'It was a nightmare for both of us.

'Kevin helped Irene rent out the house in Sutton Park. Over the course of the years while we were away, that rental income would cover the mortgage. And it was great to have the house there when we returned.

'Irene moved into my mother's house in Cabra West for that period of time. So it was difficult for them all. But it worked out well for us in the end.

'I was leaving plenty behind. Before emigrating, I was named captain of the Dublin footballers for the following year. Kevin had taken charge, and was plotting Dublin's route back to the top. He was planning for what would prove to be a hugely successful era for Dublin football on the inter-county scene.

'On a Wednesday evening, I was announced to the squad as captain. I spoke to the panel. On the Saturday, Kevin was dropping me off at Dublin Airport to start a new life.

'Things had moved quickly.

'I got word from New York to come out, that there would be work for me while I was finding my feet.

'Rather than preparing to build a team that included me, Kevin was driving me to the airport. That was the end of my county football career.'

SEÁN BOYLAN

There was always an ambition in Mickey to do what's right for his family and for himself. If he wanted to give his family an opportunity, he had to do what he did. There was no turning back.

There was no doubting about what he was after. He knew that.

Who knows what he could have added to the Dublin team in those years? He could have been the missing link against Kerry in some of those defeats.

BRIAN MULLINS

Mickey could not have achieved what he has done unless he went to America. The opportunities were there for him... he had to go. He used that as a springboard for going upwards and onwards from there.

As you can imagine, the 60s scene in Ireland around sports science wasn't very advanced. Mickey is a pioneer, and his health and well-being shows that he's still pushing the boundaries at 82 years of age.

What he achieved in America was great for him, and turned out to be great for sport in Ireland at large.

◄◄◆►►

'THERE WAS AN initial snag. When I got to the gate at departures in the airport and showed my ticket, I was told that my passport was out of date!

'I had to call Kevin from the airport.

'And Kevin called Charlie Haughey, whom he knew through GAA circles.

'Kevin had played with his brother. It was arranged that a new passport would be there for me at the passport office in Dublin, if I went straight in.

'I was able to rearrange a new flight for the next day, and I stayed with the Heffernans that night. It may sound odd. But I couldn't go home. The reason being was that I had found it so hard to leave in the first place.

'I couldn't go home and face my family again… face Irene again, because I was in bits leaving the first time. They were in bits. My parents were in bits.

'So, I knew if I went home, I'd never be able to leave. I would not be able to say goodbye a second time.

'And at the heart of it all, I wanted to make a better life for my family. I wanted to have more money to provide for them. I wanted to be a teacher.

'I did miss my family while I was away, even after Irene came out with the kids. My parents were in Ireland, as were my brother and sisters.

'But I had to keep focused on the task at hand. I needed to keep my head down and work towards my greater goal… becoming a teacher and providing for my family. I had to get the job done, and that's what I did.

'Eventually, I got on the flight at the second time of asking, with my new passport.'

'WHEN I GOT out to New York, I stayed with a Kerryman by the name of Brendan Hennessy. A gentleman, with whom I am still great friends. He invited me into his family home.

'John 'Kerry' O'Donnell was instrumental in all of this.

'It was arranged that I would be playing with the Kerry GAA club in New York. Brendan was on the team, as was his brother.

'My first job out there was manual work at a paper mill. It was mainly working night time shifts. I finished up at about 7am. It was hard work.

'That kept me going for the first few months, before I went back to working as a fitter. I got a job with a chain of supermarkets, repairing and maintaining machinery such as refrigerators, conveyer belts, escalators… lifts and lighting.

'After about five months, Irene was finally able to come out to America. We had to jump through a few hoops before she was able to cross the Atlantic.

'She was initially blocked by the American Embassy in Dublin, as they claimed I was 'moonlighting' in the United States! I didn't know I was illegal.

'I was asked to go over and I did. I had no problem getting a passport, going over and that was it. That's what I did.

'I had to find a way to get her out to America. And I did.

'John 'Kerry O Donnell helped us out.

'He had a few contacts, including crucially the Governor of New York at the time. John 'Kerry' was able to call in a favour, and the Governor was able to get onto the embassy and straighten everything out.

'They called Irene into the embassy for a meeting, and told her that everything had been ironed out. The woman who had initially told her that there was no way she could go to the U.S. turned to her and said, "Your husband must know some very important people in America!"'

MICKEY HAD ENCOUNTERED issues at the other end too.

After working in America for six months, he was told he should try to get a visa. Mickey thought it was just a case of going in and signing up. So, one day a friend brought him into the application office.

It was at the top floor of a tall building. After exiting the elevator, they both stepped into a massive open room. It was thronged.

'When I eventually got to the top of the queue, I stepped up to the counter.

'The man behind the desk was full of questions.

'What are you doing?

'Did you just arrive?'

'I explained that I had been here for six months working, and I was looking for a visa.

'He was shocked… and shaking his head, he put his right hand across on to mine and he told me… "You're not meant to be working here in the USA".

'He leaned in close, so he was out of ear-shot of anybody else. "Listen son, look around, you see all the people in this hall?' he began. "Many of them here might never work. You have a job but you're not supposed to be working here… you're illegal."

'He said he had a set of handcuffs under the counter, and it was his job to handcuff me and send me home on the next flight, but then he added… "This conversation never happened. Best of luck!"

'And he walked away.

'I did not need to be told twice! I took the hint and hurried out of there!

'My friend was sitting waiting for me, but I walked straight past him. I did not want to even wait for the elevator. I went straight for the stairs… and walked rapidly down five or six flights.'

'WHEN IRENE AND the boys eventually arrived over, and my documents were in order, we had a big party to welcome them. It was very kind of the Hennessy's, with whom I had been staying for the seven previous months.

'When Irene came, Brendan's sister Mary and her husband Jerry put us up in accommodation where we had more space for a few weeks, until we could find a place of our own.

'Each week before I moved out, I would always pay Brendan a few dollars for rent and food. It wasn't a huge amount, but I wanted to contribute.

'At the end of the party, when everybody was leaving, people were giving us cards, welcoming Irene to the country. Brendan then shook my hand and handed me an envelope. I thanked him profusely once more, and headed to the new place where we were staying.

'I assumed he had just given me a card.

'Irene was opening the envelopes when we got back to our new home.

'When she opened Brendan's… out came a wad of cash. It was all the money I had paid him over the previous few months. It included a note, saying that he didn't want this money, and it was to help us to find our feet in the U.S.

'That money gave us a real head-start. The gesture completely blew me away.

'What generosity!'

◄ ◄ ◆ ► ►

WORKING ON THE machines, Mickey was earning enough to get by.

But chatting to colleagues, he learned that wages increased once a worker became a member of a union. Naturally, he asked how he should go about signing up and getting his card. He was given an address in the city, and was given the name of someone there.

He was also given the impression that someone would be expecting him.

'The next day I was off work… I got in the car and found the place. It was a huge building, but there were barely any windows.

'I parked around the corner, walked up to the door and rang the bell. A big guy opened up. "What do you want?"'

Mickey told him who he was there to meet.

He was asked had he an appointment?

Mickey said he had. 'That's what I had thought! So, he brought me into the building, frisked me all over and then brought me down through a long corridor. We passed through two doors on the way.

'Each time, we would need to knock at a door and wait for someone to answer. I was getting an increasingly bad feeling as it went along.

'Eventually, we reached our destination. I walked into a room, and the boss man was standing with two others sitting at a table. When he heard that someone who had an appointment was coming in, he must have thought it was one of his own men.

'When I came in the two guys who were sitting reached down underneath the table. I suspect they were reaching for guns. "It's okay!" the boss said, beckoning to the two guys.

'The guys weren't taking their hands away from where they were reaching!

'The boss looked slightly unimpressed, and asked, "How the hell did you get in here?"

'Look, don't blame that man that let me in,' I told him. 'He asked me if I had an appointment, and I said I had! He then frisked me all over… brought me here to meet you.

'The Union Leader then asked me what experience I had? I gave him all my work experience, and he was impressed. He then explained to me that he believed that I was as good as any of his members but that I would have to attend classes for a year before he could give me membership.

'I thanked him, and out of that building in one piece I thought I would never get. I had heard stories, when working in the paper mill, of how the mafia would dispose of bodies. I got carried away. I was really scared.

'I got outside the door, and walked towards my car.

'But I decided to march right by it. I walked around a block before getting back in and driving away.

'I didn't drive straight home.

'I continued around for another hour. At one point, I parked and got out of the car, walked around the corner, and checked if there was anybody who had followed me.'

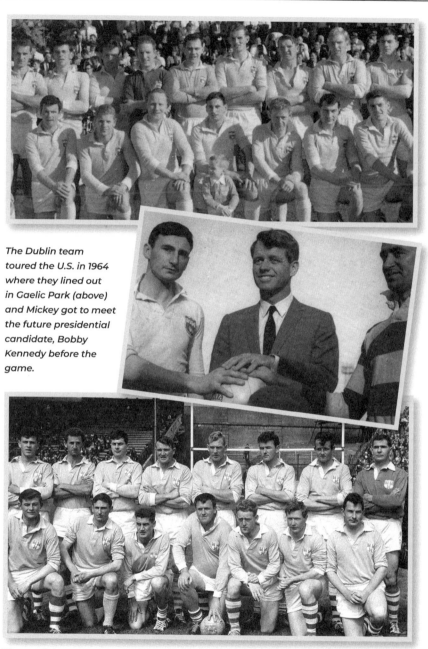

The Dublin team toured the U.S. in 1964 where they lined out in Gaelic Park (above) and Mickey got to meet the future presidential candidate, Bobby Kennedy before the game.

The good days were nearly all over for Dublin when they played Kerry in the 1965 NFL semi-final (Mickey is second from left in the front row, and Jimmy Keaveney is second from right in the back row).

« CHAPTER 11 »

SOCCER WAS A sport that opened many doors for Mickey in America, none of which he could have predicted.

While he was better known for his prowess on a gaelic football field, 'association football' was always there in the background.

Growing up, it was a sport Mickey and his friends played on the streets. There would be very few cars on the same streets. 'We would be out playing on the roads for hours and hours. It wasn't just soccer. Whatever sport was on the radio at that particular time, we wanted to emulate it!

'Soccer, basketball, cricket… you name it, we mimicked it!' Mickey's sporting appetite was also whetted at school.

'It was a long walk to St Peter's National School, and at lunchtime I would go to my grandmother's house in Phibsboro, my father's old home. In later years, when my mother stopped worrying about me making the walk, I would come home at lunchtime.

'My father had gone to that school, and knew it was a good one so he insisted that I go there. There were two local schools near me. One in Cabra, and one in Old Cabra… Christ the King, and St Finbarr's. But I went to St Peter's.'

'THE SCHOOL BACKED out onto Dalymount Park, and had a great view of the stadium. When there were cup replays or International matches played on

Wednesdays, the teachers would move the desks over to the windows facing out over the pitch. The teachers would stand behind us to watch the game as well as keeping us behaved. At that age, it was a brilliant thrill.

'Seeing these football giants playing right in front of our eyes was a great experience. There were no sheds at our end of the pitch. We could see right down to the other goalmouth. We'd be sitting up at the windows looking out, and having a better view than the large crowd that paid in.

'I was fortunate to have Paddy Woods teach me from the age of nine to 14. Every lunchtime, he would pick two teams from the class. After school we would march up to play a game of soccer on a grass area alongside the Royal Canal. Clothes and school bags acted as goalposts. The game ended when the six o'clock Angelus bell rang out from St Peter's Church. The winners would get two sums off their homework that evening. Mr Wood's team selection ensured that every student got equal time on the winning teams.

'With those high stakes, they were very competitive affairs.

'The playground in Cabra was another well organised amenity that encouraged young children to get involved with a great variation of sport and board games. At least 13 International soccer players came out of Cabra. Most, if not all, spent many enjoyable hours in the playground.

'Two of them, the brilliant Irish legend Liam Whelan, no relation, and Joe Carolan also played for Manchester United. In their schooldays they both attended St Peter's and played on successful gaelic football and hurling teams.

'In the long summer holidays after a good breakfast, I would be gone out to play on the street. We lived in 23 Drumcliffe Drive in Cabra West. This was a side-street off the main road with very little traffic. My next door neighbour was an apprentice mechanic and the only person on our street to own a car.

'Having experienced a number of balls striking his precious vehicle, he parked a short distance beyond our makeshift playing pitch on the street. We used the street to play all games… skipping, chasing… tip and tic. In the summer, listening to the radio, the BBC influence had us playing tennis during Wimbledon… and cricket if there were big games at Lords.

'Ground hurling and soccer, of course, were played there throughout the year.

'It was not long before we got the desire to develop our hurling prowess. This required travelling 200 yards to the big round-about at the top of the street. We started rolling the ball on the hurl into our hand and striking it to a partner. That was it… I was hooked.

'Very soon I was approached to play in the street league, and I never looked back.

'We'd stay out on the street until called in for our tea… then back out on the street again until bedtime.

'Another real benefit to the community of Cabra West and Old Cabra was the newly built outdoor swimming pool, which had no charge for entrance. It was well supervised and a great place to learn to swim. Myself and my friends walked a half an hour up to the pool to swim in the baths twice a day during the summer. We had great fun and most of us became strong swimmers.

'ONE EVENING, WHEN I was 14 or 15 years old, I was called in from the street. My father was sitting there with Dickie Giles… Johnny Giles' dad. Alongside them was Billy Behan, a scout from Manchester United, and my Uncle Tom.

'They wanted to bring me over to Manchester for trials.

'Billy Behan was from Ringsend. He likely saw me playing gaelic football for Clanna Gael by that stage. Or maybe he was looking out for the best players on the streets or in the playground.

'My father told me to sit down, and said, "These gentlemen want to talk to you".

'They explained that if I decided to go, they were confident I could go on to make a good living from the game. I listened to all they had to say.

'But I turned to my father and told him, "I don't want to go dad". Tears were running down my cheeks.

'He said, "That's alright son… go back out and play now".

'And that was it.

'My uncle was aghast. "He'll get rich if he goes to Manchester United!" he argued.

'When my father said, "Go out son… go out and play!" that was it. No matter if they gave him lumps of gold, he would not have taken it.

'I knew that going out the door.

'He would have been nice to them and let them down easy, but when I had my mind made up, he backed me all the way.

'The decision not to move to England at such a young age to pursue a dream of playing professional soccer was an easy one for me.

'We had lots of family members who lived in England at the time. Every Christmas and summer, they would come home and spend two weeks with us. We always had a great time together.

'They would come up to the house, and the grown-ups would have a sing-song or play cards.

'When they were all going home, everyone was crying.

'That left an awful feeling in me. When I saw my uncles and aunts going back, they were distraught.

'I couldn't take that. I didn't want to move to England.

'Do I ever wonder what might have been? *Do I have regrets?*

'Truthfully, no. It was something I just did not want to do. And I knew for certain at that age. I wouldn't have been one for going away from home. I was happy there.

'That was not the end of my soccer playing days, however.

'I never fully left the sport, in truth. I was playing bits here and there, even when I was an inter-county gaelic footballer throughout my twenties.'

WHEN MICKEY FIRST enrolled in Westchester Community College in 1970, it was quite a long commute from where the family was living. He would have to wait a couple of hours for a train into the city. Westchester Community College was in Valhalla, in upstate New York. The Whelans were living in New Jersey.

On the first day after classes, Mickey was sitting around, watching the college's soccer team train. He had a few hours to kill before he could get a train home.

'At half-time I just walked over and asked the coach if I could join in.

'I was a bit older than most of them at that stage. They were in their late-teens and early-twenties. I had a decade of inter-county football under my belt.'

The coach John Yasinac told Mickey the team had been in training for a month of pre-season and were in good shape!

Mickey told him he just wanted to train to keep himself fit.

Yasinac recognised the Irish accent, and explained that one of his best friends was from Ireland and asked Mickey did he play soccer? Mickey replied that it was a good while since he last played.

He told Mickey to bring his boots the next day and join in with them.

At half-time in the game, the coach asked Mickey was he a professional player? 'You can't play college football if you were a professional player!' he informed Mickey.

Mickey laughed and told him he had never played for any of the professional clubs in Ireland. He explained that he played a lot of gaelic football

'Oh yeah, gaelic football… my friend goes to those matches in Gaelic Park,' Yasinac stated.

He then went on to reveal what he thought was bad news.

'Unfortunately, we are not in a position to give you a scholarship because we're a public college… we can't give scholarships!'

'That's alright,' Mickey replied. 'I've already paid my fees anyway.'

'We'll have to do something about that,' the coach countered.

Yasinac signed Mickey up to play on the team that evening. He then asked to see his timetable. When Mickey was coming out of a class the following day, he approached him.

'Come with me. The president of the college wants to talk to you.' Mickey was worried… *Have I done something wrong?*

The president sat Mickey down. 'John is telling me you're a very good player, and you'd be a really good asset to the college. Unfortunately, we can't give you a scholarship.'

However, he explained they would try to make some arrangements to do something.

When Mickey arrived at training the next day, Yasinac told him the good news. 'You're getting your money back from the fees you paid!'

The refund was a massive boost for Mickey, and more importantly for his family.

MICKEY SPENT TWO years at Westchester Community College from 1970 to '72, earning a degree in Liberal Arts and Social Science. It was all with the end-goal of becoming a PE teacher.

On the soccer field, he was repaying the college's faith in him.

In the first year, the team made it to the Mid-Hudson Conference and Regional play-offs. They repeated the feat the following year, and went on to win the Mid-Hudson Conference, when Mickey captained the team.

Mickey won several individual honours. He was named as the MVP (most valuable player) on the soccer team in the college, as well as 'Outstanding College Athlete of the Year'. He was also selected to the Mid-Hudson Conference, Regional and Junior College All-American teams.

On the academic side of things, Mickey was also enjoying the journey and was getting top of the class in subjects.

After two years at Westchester Community College, however, it was time to move on. He was looking to further his studies, and specialise in PE.

He was not short on offers by this stage. Several colleges were sending him invites. They were writing, asking him to come and study. It was not only the student they wanted, they wanted a decent soccer player too!

ONE OFFER INTRIGUED him. It was from Davis and Elkins College in West Virginia. Mickey decided to go down there and check it out. John Yasinac offered to give him a lift that weekend.

It was a long drive down, and Mickey was fiddling around with the radio in John's car. As they came into West Virginia, some country music came on.

Mickey was surprised.

'That sounds like Irish music?' he said.

John explained that a lot of the West Virginia population had Irish heritage, and that was reflected in the music. Driving over picturesque mountains, listening to fiddle playing... Mickey imagined himself in Wicklow!

He had a good choice of options, but decided to go to Davis and Elkins.

Of course, that meant uprooting his family; luckily, the college could not have made it any easier. They put the Whelans up in an apartment on the campus. It was agreed that Mickey would work as a Residence Hall Director, and they would pay him for this responsibility while also providing accommodation. That eased the burden on the family.

The job did not entail a huge amount. Whenever any of the students in the house to which he was assigned had an issue, they would come to him. Be it broken lights in their accommodation, or anything that needed fixing.

'I was asked to keep an eye on any gallivanting, but there was rarely any major issue.

'My sons Shane and Cormac were four and six years old respectively when we moved to West Virginia. They loved playing in the snow. Some of the students were great with them too.

'Irene would bring them to school every day.

'Our first daughter Michelle had been born in New Jersey. So she was still young. We had Colleen then in West Virginia in 1973. The two girls still have American citizenship as a result. Our family was completed when Emma was born in 1979 back in Ireland.

'West Virginia is a beautiful part of the world.

'I loved the winter there. We never witnessed snow like we saw there. All the footpaths in the college were heated. The snow could be one foot deep on both sides of it. But there was none on the paths.

'The weather was phenomenal then during the summer. I used to bring the kids down to swim. There was a beautiful creek which was nearby, with fresh flowing water coming down from the mountains!'

OF COURSE, DURING his years in West Virginia, Mickey Whelan continued to play gaelic football, and also played hurling, for the Kerry club in New York.

He travelled up each weekend there was a match. Sometimes, that would involve flights. Other times, he drove.

'When I was flying, I would travel out of Elkins on a small plane with maybe six or eight passengers. We flew to a bigger airport in Pittsburgh and then up to New York. Some days, when it was overcast in Elkins or there was poor weather, they would announce they could not land the plane. In that case, I'd have to run out, jump in my car and drive up to the next airport.

'I would be picked up at the airport in New York and get driven to Gaelic Park. John 'Kerry' O'Donnell had a driver to bring me.

'Sometimes, I would simply drive up and down. Eight hours each way.

'A long weekend!

'But I loved being able to play gaelic football at a high level still, despite being so far from home. I competed in New York county finals out there for the Kerry club, and also lined out for the New York team.

'The GAA community in America was brilliant. During 1973, when I was in West Virginia, John 'Kerry' rang me about playing for an American invitational team against the All Stars, in both gaelic football and hurling.

'I was delighted.'

There was a catch, however! The games would be in Australia and New Zealand. The party would also be travelling to Tahiti and Fiji. A once-in-a lifetime opportunity.

However, Mickey was a full-time student. He was not in a position to just up sticks for a few weeks to travel the world during February and March.

He told John 'Kerry' that unfortunately he had to refuse the invitation.

Soon afterwards, he got a call. The president of the college wanted to see him. When Mickey arrived at his office, he was joined by the college's Head of Sport… two of the very top people at Davis and Elkins.

'Come in Michael… sit down. We just want to talk to you. We got a call from a man called John 'Kerry' O'Donnell.'

'Don't worry' I replied. 'I've already told him I'm not going on that trip. It's not feasible with my studies.'

'Relax. It's an incredible tour. If it was me… I'd give up college for it!'

'Well I'm not prepared to do that!' I responded.

'We know that, but we're going to arrange for you to get there. We've spoken to all your teachers and they have said that you are well ahead, and any classes you miss while you are away for the month… you can catch up on them in the evenings when you are back.'

They set out a programme for when Mickey returned, to compensate for the classes and exams that he would be missing.

They also gave him an assignment.

'When you're away, we want you to go to two of the Departments of Education in Australia and New Zealand, and do a project comparing their system of physical education with ours.'

This would count as credits towards Mickey's degree.

When he returned, he did all the exams that he had missed.

'I sat there on my own with each teacher.

'They also gave me lessons that I'd missed before I sat the exam. So I was busy in the evenings. I was doing the normal curriculum during the day, and then I was going back in the evening to catch up on anything I had missed.

'They were great to give their time to me. It was an incredible college. Most of the teachers lived on the campus with their families. I was massively grateful to anyone that played a part in facilitating me to go on that trip.

'It was a remarkable experience. I got to play alongside some of the greats of gaelic games, including Mick O'Connell, Niall Sheehy and Christy Ring... the three of us were playing on the U.S. selection as invitees.

'Now that was an experience.'

BY THAT STAGE, Ring was retired.

He was into his fifties. But he had not lost any of his competitive edge. He lined out for both the hurling and football teams. The party played at six venues during the tour, and Mickey also lined out in both codes for back-to-back matches on each occasion.

The hurling was first each day. Ring called Mickey and Mick O'Connell to one side at half-time in the football. 'I didn't come here to lose,' he told them.

'Every ball I get, I am going to give to you Mickey... and every ball you get Micko, give it to him too. And you Mickey... you better get scores.

'I didn't come out here to lose.'

The Cork legend still had it!

'I need not tell you, I made sure I scored every pass I received in the second-half... and we ran out winners.

'Christy was a fine footballer too. He won a county football title in 1954 with St Nicholas'.

'He didn't want to leave anything behind.

'It was a lesson that I took into my coaching career.

'What a player Ring was! And what a fascinating character. That conversation blew me away.

'That amazing man never stopped being a competitor to his dying day.'

IT WAS A memorable trip for a variety of reasons, including the homecoming. Mickey was delighted to get back to West Virginia... still alive!

'It was a bumpy ride all the way. First of all, when we landed in New York the plane burst a tyre. It was skidding from left to right on the runway.

'That was only part of it.

'When we were leaving Tahiti, it was a long-haul flight down to Auckland.

'Off we went, and everything was apparently going smoothly. But when we were about forty percent of the way there, one of the guys beside me looked out the window. He nudged me. "Hey look, Mickey. There's a fire out there!"

'It's not,' I said. 'But within moments, I realised there was in fact a fire.

'It was announced over the intercom. The right wing engine had gone on fire, and they switched it off. Nonetheless, they were going to turn around and return to Tahiti. They couldn't risk going any further.

'Everybody on the flight was with the travelling GAA party.

'When this was announced, they all had the rosary beads out. I was bricking it! It was a frightening experience. I was never so glad to get back on terra firma.

'We eventually found ourselves back in Tahiti. It was late at night by the time we landed and I thought that we would be checking into a hotel… and taking another flight the next day.

'But we were told to wait around… we would be embarking again soon.

'We disembarked and they brought us upstairs to a kind of a roof bar overlooking the whole airport. It was sweltering hot.

'We were on this roof, and we were all agreeing… *I don't see any other plane coming to pick us up!*

'Someone eventually enquired. And they told us we would be getting back onto the plane we had already been on.

'We could make out that our plane was half a mile away on the runway.

'Suddenly, the night sky lit up. It looked like the plane had caught fire!

'A few minutes later, there was an announcement to say we'd be embarking on the plane in another couple of minutes. We had to get ready.

'We were all worried.

'One of our guys went to our management. "That plane is after igniting out there… it blew up!" he stated.

'He was told he was wrong. "No, what happened was it had burst a pipe… that's why the engine went on fire. They do that to get all the oil off the engine and the plane. We light it up… to burn off all the excess."

'Considering how brightly it had been burning, we thought the whole plane had exploded.

'But they said there was no problem.

'So we got onto the plane anyway.

'It was late at night. People were tired… half were asleep.

'After about three or four hours, just over halfway through the journey this time, the engine went on fire again.

'The rosary beads all came out again… fast.

'It was even more worrying this time around!

'The captain came on!'

'We're over halfway there… so we're going to go on!' he stated.

'I was thinking to myself, between a punctured tyre on the first flight and now engines exploding… *I'm doomed!*

'We eventually got there, touching down in Auckland. People were crying… hugging each other in relief. But, if I didn't have enough near-death experiences on that trip, there was to be one more!

'WE WERE STAYING in a hotel in Sydney for a week. I came down for breakfast one morning, and everybody was looking at me. I thought there was something hanging off the back of me, because of all the attention I was drawing.

'I was looking around.

'John 'Kerry' came over to me. "Where were you last night?"

'I was in bed, John!'

'You couldn't have been in bed… there was an earthquake. The hotel was completely evacuated!'

'This was news to me! Maybe it was all the jet-lag and fatigue from travelling, but I had a sound night's sleep.

'I didn't believe them at first.

'I sat down with John's wife. She explained that they were evacuated. They were looking at the building from the outside. It was a tall hotel, and it shook… moving the beds across the floor. After a few hours when everything had calmed down, they were eventually let back into their rooms.

'I had not noticed a thing. I had just rolled out of bed that morning. But when I got back to my room, I realised the bed had moved across to the other side of the room during the night!'

AFTER TWO YEARS in West Virginia, Mickey graduated from Davis and Elkins. At this stage, Irene was eager to get home to Ireland.

When he graduated, however, he still felt he needed another string to his academic bow. He asked Irene if she'd mind if they waited another year?

Mickey wanted to do a Masters degree.

Irene agreed to one more year.

Mickey found West Virginia University, where he would study a Masters of Science.

The university was in Morganstown, which was over an hour's drive from Davis and Elkins. However, they were well settled as a family in Davis and Elkins, so Mickey commuted over and back across that year.

He also stayed working in Davis and Elkins, and helped to coach the soccer team. That helped the family stay afloat financially. They were happy with Mickey's contribution, and wanted him to stay on the year afterwards, so he could take over as Head Coach.

But, it was time for the family to go home. That didn't stop Davis and Elkins asking. Even after the family moved back to Ireland, he was asked for three years in-a-row if he would return.

'At one point a few years later, I decided I would go back to the States for a while. I handed in my notice at my teaching job in Dublin, and was all set to move. However, I couldn't bring myself to leave. I wasn't able to tear myself apart from Irene and the kids once again.

'The Masters in West Virginia was the last of my studies for quite some time. When I returned, I went down to Limerick to investigate the possibility of doing a PhD at Thomond College. I was informed they had only recently opened the programme, and they couldn't yet facilitate a PhD student. I could have done a Masters degree, but I already had one.

'It wasn't feasible, but I promised myself I would do a PhD when I retired.'

And Mickey did manage to do that… in his seventies in DCU.

DURING THAT TIME in West Virginia, Mickey also played professional soccer. It wasn't big money, but it was nonetheless a good standard.

He lined out with the Connecticut Wildcats.

An ex-Davis and Elkins player recommended him. Mickey played a number of games for them in the American Soccer League.

One of the biggest games for the Wildcats was against the Argentine club Estudiantes de La Plata. Club teams didn't come much bigger than the

Argentinians at the time. They had won three consecutive Copa Libertadores in 1968, '69 and '70. They also won the Intercontinental Cup in 1968, a precursor for today's FIFA Club World Cup, in which they beat European champions Manchester United in the final.

Unfortunately, the day before the Wildcats were due to play the South American giants, Mickey injured ligaments playing a football match at Gaelic Park! That put him out of action for the rest of the season. They didn't operate… just telling him to rest. Nevertheless, the match programme listed a few notes on each player:

Mickey Whelan.

Fullback.

Elkins, WV.

5'10", 170 pounds.

One of the best all-round players ever to play at Westchester Community College or Davis and Elkins College, Mickey is expected to be the bulwark of the Wildcats' defence this season. A Junior College All American both years at Westchester, Mickey was named to All Conference, All Tournament, and All American teams at Davis and Elkins in 1972 and 1973, becoming only a handful of four-time All Americans.

EVENTUALLY, IT WAS time to move home.

Mickey wasn't entirely finished with his Masters degree, as there were still aspects he needed to complete in Dublin. 'Physical fitness of Dublin 16-year-old schoolboys compared to Americans of same sex and age'… that was the title of his Masters project. The Whelans came back to their house in Sutton Park. The next issue was the small matter of getting a job. Good fortune would look after that.

Three days after they arrived home, Mickey was doing a weekly food shop at the supermarket.

'Mickey, how are you?' said William Purcell, a Tipperary man he knew, who was the principal in Killester Vocational School.

Before Mickey had gone away, he had done a small bit of basketball coaching there, which he was roped into doing by Kevin Heffernan.

'You're home now? You're permanently home now?' William asked. 'And you have a degree?'

Mickey explained what he had studied throughout his time in America.

'I think I'll have a part-time position for you!' The Department of Education had just qualified their first class of physical education teachers and the demand for PE was huge. The first PE teachers were gobbled up and there was hundreds of schools disappointed, including Killester Vocational School

'He required a teacher with physical education in his degree, because there was only one PE teacher and they needed two as the student numbers were rapidly expanding,' Mickey says. *Just by the grace of God.*

'You attended the Technical School in Cabra West, did you not?'

'I did indeed, Mr Purcell,' Mickey replied.

William also asked, 'So you did metalwork and technical drawing?

'Yes.'

'I need some of your hours to be in metalwork, alongside your science classes in order to hire you as a part-time teacher.'

'It's been a long time since I did metalwork,' Mickey told him. 'It was one of the subjects I enjoyed as a student'.

William said his Vice-Principal, Mr Corish was a metal work teacher and he would help Mickey go through the metalwork programme a week before school opened.

Mickey was in a temporary position for almost a year. At the end of that year, he applied to the Department of Education for a full-time position. He was called for interview and was successful. He taught there for 10 happy years, fully involved in all the sports and teaching science and PE subjects.

The family's future was now a brighter one.

'Granted, I was starting on the lowest rung of the teaching ladder.

'But it proved that moving to America for my studies was the right decision at the time for me and my family.'

When he moved to the U.S. in 1969 to study, Mickey took a change of direction by concentrating on soccer, lining out with Davis and Elkins Community College and also Westchester CC.

He still continued to play gaelic football at weekends in New York and was fortunate to get to tour Australia and New Zealand and the South Sea Islands in the early 70s with some amazing company, including the legendary pair of Christy Ring (front row, far left) and Mick O'Connell (front row, third from left).

« CHAPTER 12 »

PAT GILROY

In 2010, the learning curve caught up on us. We were learning so fast throughout that summer, taking the qualifier route, we probably just didn't have the resources right throughout the team.

Physically, we were playing a high-intensity game. We maybe died in that last 10 or 15 minutes against Cork. They were just superior to us. They were a better team at that time. But I felt with another winter's training, we would catch up on them and overtake them. And the National League in 2011 certainly showed that we had closed that gap. We beat Cork comfortably in the league phase. While they overcame us in the final, I wasn't too worried about losing that.

I felt that had we won in the league final, we might not have had the hunger to go on and win the All-Ireland. I wasn't that upset about losing it, even though we shouldn't have lost it.

We were eight points up, and we made mistakes from the sideline, maybe putting in inexperienced guys when we needed to close out the game. Maybe we should have put in some of the older guys. But I think we learned a lot from the mistakes we made in that loss, both as management and players. And we rectified that when we got to those positions in the championship.

◄◄◆►►

THE PROGRESS DUBLIN made in 2010 boosted confidence and expectations. They had gone toe-to-toe with the eventual All-Ireland champions.

It started out as a three-year project. But Dublin very nearly scaled the peak after year two.

'There were not many changes left to do,' Mickey explains. 'By this stage we knew we had the personnel with the right attitude and mentality. We were going to back the players that we had, and they were doing the job.

'While there might not have been as great a rebuilding job to do compared to the previous winter, it wasn't as if we were going to let the players off the hook. We couldn't afford to stand still, or we would have been overtaken.

'We knew we had to work them hard, to build up a solid base level of fitness throughout the off-season.'

In that regard, the National League in 2011 was not about building or finding out about the team. It was about winning.

Dublin hit the ground running straight away, winning their first six matches in Division 1. That included a win over Kerry at Croke Park, 3-10 to 1-15. The teams had not met in the previous championship campaign, but Dublin wanted to double down on their 2010 victory in Killarney.

Dublin drew with Galway in their last game, having already been assured of a place in the final. Beating the top teams in the country that springtime only furthered belief.

'You don't just win a championship on the last day. It's a longer process than that. You have to get them playing together, believing in themselves, and we had to know that if there's something going wrong... *Who can we bring in?* You're all the time looking for the players to be better and better.'

Dublin also beat Cork, 3-13 to 0-16 during that run, with Mossy Quinn, Kevin McManamon and Barry Cahill all finding the net.

In the final, they came up against the Rebels once more.

However, Cork came back from an eight-point deficit to win 0-21 to 2-14. Dublin were moving in the right direction, but were not yet the finished article.

Pat Gilroy was asked about the team's character by the media, and backed his men to the hilt.

This team has more character and more guts to put up with the kind of stuff that surrounds them every day. And they get back out there and they train and they work.

And I tell ya... they are the most honest guys.

They will get stick for this. It was an eight-point lead and they lost. We have to deal with that. Because that is our job. We are the Dublin team and we have to listen to that.

And when we have the All-Ireland someday... that is when we will stop hearing that. That's the challenge. Because that's what everyone is going to think but I know what's in that dressing-room. They have serious character and anyone who questions it, well, they might get a surprise. Someday.

But in fairness, that question is well asked and it is going to be asked every day for the next two months and it is up to us to answer it during the summer.

It is as simple as that.

THE MANAGEMENT TEAM didn't see the loss as a setback. They were able to harness the disappointment to get even more work done with the players.

Focus quickly turned to the upcoming Leinster Championship campaign. Dublin were still hurting after what happened the previous summer in the province. Regaining the Delaney Cup was going to be crucial.

'You want to win everything. It's as simple as that. Every game you play, every competition you enter, you're going out to win.

'Of course, what do you want to win the most? The All-Ireland final. So you're building for the All-Ireland final all the time. And it's about raising the levels. No matter how well they play in the Leinster final, you're still putting them under pressure to be even better for the next match.

'You get to the stage with a group like that when they have fully bought into the team ethos. There's a stage where these lads start driving themselves.

'When they know there is another man gunning to take their place, they have to get that mentality themselves.

'The main thing we needed to make sure was that they had the fitness and the ability. We kept working on getting more out of them; improving their abilities, sometimes unknown to themselves through training drills. We really worked them hard, and it was beginning to pay off.

'That laid the foundations for the successes this team would go on to achieve in the intervening years. Confidence breeds confidence. The more they won, the more they knew they were going to win.

'They believed in themselves.'

BRYAN CULLEN WAS chosen as captain that year. There were plenty of leaders on the team all over the pitch. But Cullen was a cool customer.

And he read the game well.

'You need to have a leader in every line if possible. He was central to everything, and always kept his feet on the ground.

'The tradition from my playing days where the county champions selected the Dublin senior football captain was long gone. And as a management team, it was important that we could choose the player we felt would be the greatest asset for the group as a whole.

'Bryan was the type of player who could do anything. He was seen more as a half-back when we arrived, but his fielding ability made him an ideal candidate for the half-forward line.

'He could even play in goals! I was a selector on the Ireland International Rules team in 2005 for the tour of Australia, and we put Bryan in the nets. He was able to come out with the ball and pick a pass.

'Fortunately, we did not have to consider handing him the No 1 jersey for Dublin, as we had the best in the business in Stephen Cluxton.'

Pete McGrath, who guided Down to two All-Ireland titles, was the Ireland manager for that trip Down Under. Mickey Linden and Larry Tompkins were also coaches.

The GAA president at the time, Seán Kelly asked Mickey to join the backroom team too. It was a fascinating prospect, and once Irene gave him the green light, he was thrilled to agree.

'I found International Rules to be a cross-breed of a game, being honest. Two sports were squashed into one.

'We were coming up against professional athletes, and they milled us. It was a physical contest, and they came out on top. They won the first test 100-64, and the second 63-42. But it was still an enjoyable experience working with the top players from all over Ireland.'

◄◄◆►►

TAKING THE QUALIFIER route in 2010 brought with it some inadvertent benefits. But in 2011 Dublin felt they needed to go the direct course.

Laois were first up in the Leinster Championship quarter-final, and it was a challenge they managed to brush aside.

◄ ◄ ◆ ▷ ►

2011 LEINSTER SFC QUARTER-FINAL
DUBLIN 1-16 LAOIS 0-11

We didn't really learn anything we didn't already know. Dublin boast some sweet-footed forwards with Alan Brogan and Diarmuid Connolly in the thick of it this time, and Bernard Brogan also showing up as usual despite the very close attention of Cahir Healy. Bryan Cullen suddenly has a ferocious appetite for football again, and Dublin's calm and efficient defence can handle the simple stuff very well.

Laois had tested them, alright, but hardly as thoroughly or truly as some teams waiting down the line will – starting no doubt with Kildare in the Leinster semi-final, back in Croke Park.

◄ ◄ ◆ ▷ ►

KILDARE WERE A step up in opposition, and had been improving under Kieran McGeeney. They were unlucky not to have reached the All-Ireland final the previous year.

Dublin led by six at half-time, 1-7 to 0-4.

A late Bernard Brogan free saw off a Kildare fightback to steer Dublin into the Leinster final. It was a tough game, and Kildare providing such a strong challenge was a massive help. The harder the games, the better for Gilroy, Whelan and Co. Wexford provided the opposition in the final.

Dublin won by a single goal.

◄ ◄ ◆ ▷ ►

2011 LEINSTER SFC FINAL
DUBLIN 2-12 WEXFORD 1-12

Arguably the biggest shock at Croke Park yesterday wasn't the sight of Wexford unnerving Dublin, but rather the realisation that Bernard Brogan is human after all.

The reigning Footballer of the Year is the most lethal weapon in the Dublin armoury.

And it looked like the start of a routine day at the office when he spectacularly curled over a point from a tight angle after only 20 seconds. But a combination of stout Wexford defending and uncharacteristic wayward finishing would dominate his afternoon from then on, with Brogan taken off 10 minutes from time.

Pat Gilroy replaced his entire starting full-forward line, with Diarmuid Connolly called ashore early and Eoghan O'Gara off at half-time with a wrist injury.

◄◄◆►►

JAMES MCCARTHY SCORED a goal, while Denis Bastick, Paul Flynn, Bryan Cullen, Kevin McManamon and Ross McConnell all contributed to the haul.

Bernard Brogan was the reigning Footballer of the Year, but had a quiet day by his standards. It showed the importance of building a strong squad.

It was key to have an array of players who were capable of contributing meaningful scoring tallies. At that stage, there were at least 20 lads who could have started on the Dublin team. The first-leg of the job was done, as Dublin had returned to the All-Ireland series with the Leinster title.

They would face Tyrone in the All-Ireland quarter-final for the second consecutive year. Having knocked them out 12 months beforehand, and relegated them to Division 2 in 2010, Dublin were confident.

'You never quite have another team's number. But you can go into a game with the belief that if you play your best, you are going to win no matter what. You can't forecast it. I was long enough in the game to know that. There were times there that we lost games we should have won.

'In that regard, you have to warn against complacency. You just have to get them to the mental pitch. We had brought them to the stage where they were physically able to stay going forever, no matter who they were playing or how hard it got. They were going to be as good at the end of a match as they were at the beginning.

'That was an important aspect, as many teams would wane.

'This team had the ability, and they had learned how to win by themselves.

'That's something you cannot teach.

'They had a feel for each other on the field, as they had now been playing and building together for three years. We could see they were developing, able to read each other's movements. The work we were doing on the training field all helped with that… all ball work.

'But having said all of that, you needed to be right mentally to avoid any slip-ups.'

Dublin backed up those previous victories against Tyrone, winning by seven points on a wet night at Croke Park. Diarmuid Connolly ran riot, kicking points from all over the field. He finished with seven points from play.

'It was one of Diarmuid's greatest performances for Dublin. He was a brilliant player, for both club and county. As a minor it was clear he had what it takes. He was very young on the team I managed at St Vincent's, but was brilliant in our run to the All-Ireland Club Championship.

A guy who could do anything with the ball.

◄◄◆►►

2011 ALL-IRELAND SFC QUARTER-FINAL
DUBLIN 0-22 TYRONE 0-15

Dublin blew Tyrone away with an irresistible display of power football to book an All-Ireland SFC semi-final date with Donegal.

Pat Gilroy's inspired team produced a marvellous performance of committed, controlled endeavour to blast their way through to the last four.

Diarmuid Connolly led the way with a marvellous seven-points tally, all from play. Indeed, the Dubs hit 19 scores from play, and although they failed to find the net, they could have had three goals on a night when they never looked like being beaten.

◄◄◆►►

IT WAS BEGINNING to click, but there was a major challenge coming down the tracks. Donegal were Ulster champions, and were emerging under Jim McGuinness as a real force. They were bringing something different, packing their defence and making it difficult for opposition teams to score.

Dublin knew exactly how they were going to set up. The problem was that a lot of teams did, but still couldn't come up with any solutions.

Dublin decided to tweak their preparations.

'We had seen how Donegal committed numbers back when the opposition had the ball. And they would pour forward with pace when they won possession.

'So how could we be ready?

'At our training matches, we decided we would play 15 vs 18. That would prepare our lads to play against a disproportionate number of players in a certain area of the field.

'We wanted our six forwards to be able to handle nine defenders. We wanted our six backs to be able to handle their nine forwards when they were storming up the field. In the training match, we might even throw one extra body in against the team of 15 without announcing it to the group. It would teach them to adapt to the situation and come up with a solution.

'We also had to warn against the temptation to pour forward.

'Donegal had shown how good they were on the turnover and how dangerous they were on the break. They could hurt us.'

◄◄◆►►

ALAN BROGAN

When we were playing training matches, Mickey used to put in extra defenders. It made sense, because that's what we were going to be up against playing Donegal. To be fair to him and Pat, they were very tactically astute, and thought about what was coming down the line. With that game coming, we knew that Donegal were going to have a lot of men behind the ball. So they set the training sessions that way.

It was a very difficult couple of weeks leading into it. And at times, it was disheartening! As a forward in the lead-up to a match, you like to play a couple of games, get your hands on the ball and kick a few scores to get your confidence up.

Games which you usually enjoyed… and all of a sudden, six of us forwards were playing against nine or 10 defenders. It was gruelling. He obviously prepared us very well for what lay ahead in that game. It was another sign of how well Mickey and Pat prepared the team, and how forward-thinking they were in terms of getting the team prepared for what was coming down the line.

◄◄◆►►

DUBLIN KNEW THEY were facing into a war of attrition.

In truth, Dublin ended up beating Donegal at their own game. It was far from a classic. But it was a case of 'horses for courses'.

'I have never been involved in a match like it. You would often have a man back to give more cover. Instead of just two midfielders for kick-outs and that, we always had two wing forwards to drop back to help and give an option.

'But this was a different level altogether.

'They led 0-4 to 0-2 at half-time. Awful stuff.

'But we sat back and they couldn't get through us. We ended up coming out on top, 0-8 to 0-6. Two points was a significant winning margin in that particular game, given the circumstances.

'It was all about getting through the match with a win. We would have taken a 0-1 to 0-0 scoreline! It proved that we were able to adapt. Dublin would be willing to play a variety of ways, but still come out with a victory.

'We only scored two points from play. It must have been awful to look at for the neutrals.

'The thing about it was... Donegal expected us to play our normal game. So they thought they would be flushing guys forward and over-running our defence. But we were sitting back waiting for them.

'It screwed them up... it screwed the game up, but it meant we were through to an All-Ireland final... our first in 16 years.'

Of course, with that came some unavoidable hype.

AN ALL-IRELAND FINAL is no ordinary game. The build-up is different. And as a management team, Pat Gilroy and his men had to try and shield the players from all of that as much as they could.

The players were warned against some traps early on.

'If there are tickets you need to sort for your friends and family or whatever, it all has to be done in one day.

'Get rid of them... you're not talking to anybody else after that!'

The management team couldn't have players scrambling around, sorting tickets for different people every night of the week. If they had to sort five different people out with tickets, they needed to meet all those five people on the one evening. And that was it.

Distractions like that couldn't be going on for two weeks. It had to be gone and out of their heads. It was all very professional. The players took it in their stride.

It had shown how far the team had come as a group. There were no longer any trepidations about playing outside Leinster in knockout matches in the All Ireland series.

'You cannot fully play down the significance of an All-Ireland final. But how we prepared them was, we upped the significance of every time they stepped out onto the field.

'Every player's position was up for grabs in every training match, and they had to play that way. We had made big decisions over the course of the three years by dropping players. So they knew these weren't empty threats.

'But by playing with such pressure on their shoulders every day they went out, they became accustomed to it.'

It was a frantic build-up, but also a fruitful one.

'An All-Ireland final is a massive deal. The preparation is all business. There is a job to be done. When it is over and you succeed, that is when you can enjoy it.

'We did not focus as much on Kerry as we had on Donegal. We needed to concentrate on our own game. Of course, we would always have a talk about their threats and how we could stymie them, while also looking how to best expose any weaknesses they might have.

'Midfield was always going to be important to win. Kerry always dominated midfield… that had been the source from where their forwards got the right service.

'We had learned that it was a key battleground in our two wins over them in the last two National League campaigns.

'Our two wing half-forwards Paul Flynn and Bryan Cullen were both great fielders. Bryan read the game really well and never gave the ball away. Paul was also a brilliant player. He could go forward and score.

'It was a great combination.

'They would come back into midfield to help win the 50-50s. Any ball we won, they would strike at pace. We did a lot of work on that.

'Those two previous wins over Kerry were huge. It built our belief… especially going down there and winning. Kerry do not like to be beaten anywhere, at any time, in any match.

'Taking over the job in late-2008, we always knew the Kingdom were going to be the standard-bearers. In order to win an All-Ireland, we would likely need to go through them at some point.

'That has always been the way, even going back to my own playing career.

'In 2011, we felt we were able for them.'

DUBLIN WERE A better team in 2011 than they had been in 2010. They were another year on, playing together.

The team had the benefit of one added year working on a game-plan, and management were throwing in new challenges in training. The team's fitness was never higher. Mickey believed the lads would run forever.

'We were doing training at the top level. We were going to outlast any opposition. In the quarter-final and semi-final, we finished far stronger than our opposition.

'On the training field, we worked them harder than ever.

'We would be training for two hours. Firstly, we would warm-up really well, do flexibility… stepping over hurdles, standing over them… hopping over them.

'Then we would move into a match, with maybe a five-minute break for half-time. We got to the stage where three-quarters of the way into a game, they might be beginning to tire.

'I took them out, and they had to solo 30 yards fast… hand-pass off to a guy standing at the bottom of the hill… then they had to fly up the hill.

'We would have someone on the hill roaring at them.

'I always feel it is important to incorporate the ball into a drill, so you're used to concentrating on possession when you're going at full tilt.

'This was all after maybe 90 minutes of hard work.

'And I'd tell them, "Listen fellas, we're going back in there now for the next 15 minutes. And if you don't do it here, you won't do it on game-day!"

'Simple as that.

'And they got back in. I'd run the stuffing out of them, climbing up maybe 12 or 14 feet high gradients, over maybe 30 yards. It was a sprint uphill. But they were sprinting while soloing.

'And before that, we might have done a few sprints without the ball, where they'd have to go flat out.

'There was no slacking.

'Even the man who knew he wasn't going to be in the starting 15 wanted to be with the group. They knew they were going places… *This team is going to win here and I want to be part of it, even if I might not be starting.*

'That's what they were thinking.'

◄◄◆►►

ALAN BROGAN

In training sessions, Mickey had a great way of focusing fellas on the field. If he was training you, you wouldn't want to let him down. He thrived on fellas giving their all, and pushing the boat out. There was no session where he'd let the standards drop, and if he spotted anything… many a time I saw him calling out fellas who were maybe taking shortcuts or not putting as much effort in. So he really got the most out of fellas.

And that's a difficult thing to do as a coach, because there's only so much shouting and roaring you can do before fellas stop responding to it. But the way Mickey had about him, the guys always responded to it. He kept a little bit of distance from the players. For instance, he wouldn't come to too many of the after-match functions and stuff. He might show his face and have a bite to eat, but he'd be gone after that. Whereas some of the management team might have hung around and had a few beers.

He probably felt that was important. If he wanted to get the most out of guys and give guys a rollicking, he didn't want to be too close to them.

At the training sessions, he wasn't afraid to let lads have it if he had to. In a respectful manner. I don't think you'd hear a bad word about Mickey from anyone in that team.

He had the best interests of the players at heart. And he had the best interests of Dublin football at heart all the time.

NIALL MOYNA

Pat changed the culture of that Dublin team, there's no doubt about that. But Mickey Whelan set the standards. Dublin would not have won that All-Ireland in 2011 if Mickey was not on board. There's no doubt in my mind.

I think the legacy he left with Dublin going for five-, six- and seven-in-a-row was phenomenal. And those players still love Mickey to this day..

◄◄◆►►

'OVER THE COURSE of the season, we were flying. And that was going to be crucial when we were up against Kerry, going down the final straight.

'If Kerry were going to beat us, they would have had to be well clear. We knew that if we were within touching distance when the game was turning for home, we would finish strong.

'Our guys weren't going to be found wanting for fitness. They were going to be able to play, right up at the pace they were at… right up to the end.'

The final whistle was mayhem. As were the following few hours.

It was magical for everyone, including the management team.

For Mickey, 2011 was the icing on the cake.

Kevin McManamon's brilliant goal and Stephen Cluxton's equally amazing match-winning point got Dublin over the line against Kerry in the 2011 All-Ireland final.

With Bryan Cullen lifting Sam, Dublin were finally back as the No 1 football team in the country and no group of players deserved it more. The backroom team (above) also worked its socks off and deserved to share in the glory in the privacy of their dressing-room.

« CHAPTER 13 »

KEVIN HEFFERNAN ALWAYS told Mickey Whelan that you never stop coaching.

You never retire.

Always keep giving back. It is a message Mickey passed on to Pat Gilroy.

In 2019, Pat and Mickey managed St Vincent's to the Dublin under-21 'B' Football Championship.

More recently, Mickey has been managing the club's senior camogie team. In the truncated 2020 season, Vincent's reached the county senior camogie final, only to lose to St Jude's. They won the county title in 2019, and went on to claim the Leinster club title.

Pat Gilroy worked with the team too for the 2021 season.

'Pat remained on as Dublin senior football manager after my departure in 2011. I looked on from afar in 2012, as Dublin tried to defend the All-Ireland title. I was on record after 2011 as saying that this team would go on to win five All-Irelands. Not necessarily in-a-row.

'But they would go on and achieve huge success.

'I looked at the likes of Stephen Cluxton, Michael Fitzsimons, Cian O'Sullivan, James McCarthy, Michael Darragh Macauley, Paul Flynn, Bernard Brogan and so many more.

'They helped Dublin dominate over the following years, as they achieved eight

All-Irelands in 10 years. I was never going to be involved in 2012, as I wanted to spend more time with Irene. But nonetheless I was a keen observer from afar.'

◄◄◆►►

TOMÁS 'MOSSY' QUINN

I felt Mickey was a big loss in 2012. I suppose you have to caveat it with it being the year after winning it for the first time in 16 years, and everything that went with it.

So it was probably a number of different factors.

But it was definitely a factor. Mickey had us so finely tuned physically.

2012 was a different challenge. I don't know if we celebrated too much. But previously we were coming into it with a freshness and a hunger. And there's that kind of manic-ness to do what you needed to get over the line.

Whereas it's probably a different challenge for guys in the second year. And we knew it deep down… we put in hard training, but we were probably a little bit off.

I remember we did a training camp down in Kerry, before the Mayo semi-final. And I think they felt we were a little bit off the pace after the Leinster Championship and All-Ireland quarter-final, and we did savage training down in Kerry, which was only 10 days or two weeks out from the semi-final.

I actually remember a couple of people were even thinking… I don't know if we'd have done that if Mickey was there.

We probably wouldn't have been in the situation where we felt we were off the pace. That's not to say we didn't have some savage sessions with Mickey a week out from a game or two weeks out.

I'm sure the people making the decisions at the time, from a sports science point of view, could back it all up. And it's easy in hindsight – if we'd beaten Mayo, we would have looked back and said, 'That was a great training weekend'.

But obviously when you lose, there's different questions asked. But he was definitely missed around the place.

PAT GILROY

You couldn't argue with Mickey stepping away after 2011. There was a personal situation. Irene wasn't well. He wanted to spend time with her.

And it was totally the right decision. To be honest, I intended on stepping away as well after 2011. It was ninety percent a 'No', and I told the County Board that within a week of the All-Ireland. I didn't think I'd go on. Ah, I suppose people badgered me into it, when I probably didn't really want to do it in 2012.

Work was getting very busy overseas.

I ended up doing a lot of travel, landing back from America at 5am and going to a training session that night. I didn't have the same flexibility work-wise that I had the previous three years.

I enjoyed 2012, but it was hard without Mickey. You were kind of hoping that he would come back, and maybe Irene would recover and get better. But it didn't happen. We got on with it, we gave it a fair crack.

But I definitely decided 2012 was going to be my last year right from the start. I don't regret doing it, because I enjoyed it. They did give it a great lash that year. They got very close to beating Mayo in that semi.

But what has happened since has been fantastic as well.

It was strange in 2012 without Mickey. We were able to do a lot of the same stuff because we had been around him so long at that stage. You try to keep a lot of the same stuff, and maybe add a few bits and pieces.

We would stay in touch… Niall Moyna and I would meet him the odd time to get a bit of advice. But his time was focused elsewhere, and rightly so. It was tough, because we had worked so closely together.

To take him out of it, there was a big gap and a big hole to fill.

I think Niall Moyna did an incredible job training them, because he replicated so much of what Mickey had done. And we were unlucky. Had Bernard Brogan's shot gone in against Mayo, maybe we would have gone on and won that All-Ireland.

But that's sport. It's fine margins.

◄◄◆▷►

'I STILL WENT to the games. It was a strange feeling, not being able to make decisions during matches.

'But I was happy to live with my decision to walk away.

'Pat stepped down after 2012. He is very successful in his work, and could no longer invest the required time.'

It looked like the pair would not work together again on the national stage.

But that all changed in late 2017. Mickey was on holiday in Portugal when his phone rang. It was Pat. He explained that he had been offered the Dublin hurling job.

'That's great, Pat... congratulations. You should give that a shot!'

'But I wouldn't do it without you. You'd come in with me... wouldn't you?'

'Ah Jaysus! Pat!'

Pat said, 'No, I wouldn't do it unless you came in!'

They talked it over for 30-odd minutes. And Pat talked Mickey into it.

They were afraid the public and more importantly the team might see them as a 'gaelic football management team', coming in to coach the hurlers.

Pat coerced Mickey into it, and he invited Anthony Cunningham on board - Cunningham had brought Galway to two All-Ireland finals in 2012 and '15.

◄◄◆►►

PAT GILROY

The Dublin hurling job in 2018 was something that kind of came out of the blue for me. They were struggling to find someone. I don't think Mattie Kenny was a proper option, because Cuala were looking like they were going to go on (competing in the All-Ireland Club Championship) to March.

They were flying along. The County Board wanted to stabilise things. I was always interested, and I love hurling.

It probably wasn't the right time for me work-wise. I was a bit busy, but I took it on anyway. We made a fair crack of it. I think we stabilised it a bit, and got them back on the straight and narrow. I would have liked to do it a bit longer, but sometimes work has to dictate these things, and that's how your bills are paid. So we didn't probably get out of it as much as we would have liked.

Mickey was worried about us not being seen as hurling people. We felt having Anthony Cunningham there was important. None of us had coached hurling for a long time. Even Paddy O'Donoghue, who had been on the football management team with us... we had all played hurling to a decent standard.

It would have been years since we were doing it at a high level though.

So having Anthony was invaluable. He brought an awful lot.

Himself and Mickey got on great together. We had Seán Brady there in the background, who had played senior hurling for Dublin. Those three did a lot of the coaching, and they did a great job on it.

◄ ◄ ◆ ▷ ►

2018 WAS NOT the first time Mickey had worked with the Dublin hurlers.

He had played club hurling throughout his career, although it was limited by Kevin Heffernan, who insisted they should concentrate on the big ball. That didn't prevent Mickey from playing in successful junior and intermediate club hurling finals when a member of Clanna Gael Fontenoys,

He played hurling in the U.S., and even got roped into lining out for St Vincent's hurlers on one occasion. He was washing his car outside his home in Sutton Park; he had just finished soaping the car and had washed down one side when his wife brought out his phone to him. His great friend Tony Diamond was on the other end of the line issuing a directive to get into the car immediately and drive to the club.

'It was near half-time and a player had just come off the field injured, and they had no subs. It was a junior club final and they would lose the game if they could not field a full team on the restart. I immediately dropped everything and drove to the club… changed into jersey and shorts, and fielded on the restart.

'I had not played hurling for 10 years… but scored a point. We won the game, but I was more concerned about the suds damaging my car.

'I helped out the training with the club's senior side in the 80s, before Lar Foley took over the Dublin senior hurlers in 1989. Lar was a huge name in Dublin hurling, having played in an All-Ireland final in 1961. There was real talent in the county when he took over, and I was invited on board.'

A Leinster quarter-final defeat to Laois ensured the 1989 campaign was a case of 'one-and-done', but the O'Moore County were no push-overs at the time.

Though 1990 was more successful, as Dublin reached the Leinster final after a semi-final win over Wexford, 2-16 to 1-17.

Offaly ran out five-point winners in the final, 1-19 to 2-11.

It was a defeat Dublin would avenge the following year, edging them 0-19 to 1-14. However, Kilkenny narrowly won the decider, 1-13 to 1-11. Dublin were coming close to the country's top teams those years in Leinster, but were narrowly missing out on a major breakthrough.

Unfortunately, it did not quite happen. The knockout nature of the championship was cruel. One slip-up and it was over for another year.

Mickey stayed with the group when Lar departed.

'It was a pleasure to coach alongside him. Jimmy Gray came in, and I worked with the panel for another few years until the footballers came calling for me to take over as manager.

'John Bailey, the County Board chairman at the time, asked Jimmy's permission before approaching me for the football job.'

THERE IS NO reason why Dublin cannot be competing at the very top level in both hurling and football, in Mickey's estimation… and challenging for All-Ireland titles every year.

'The current squad is knocking on the door. I believe they are not far away from a significant breakthrough.

'Huge progress was made under Anthony Daly. The National League and Leinster Championship titles were fully deserved. They should have reached the All-Ireland final in 2013, and I think they would have won had they beaten Cork in that semi-final.

'It was a hugely exciting prospect taking charge alongside Pat and Anthony.

'Three years has often done the trick when I took over teams. St Vincent's and Dublin both clicked in year three. We were looking at the Dublin hurlers as a similar project.

'Having worked together previously, Pat and I looked to apply some of the same principles which had worked for us throughout our time with the footballers.

'Firstly, we wanted to scour the county for talent. We didn't want to just inherit a panel. We wanted to build our own.'

Conal Keaney was one whom they felt still had much to offer. Though well into his thirties by that stage, he was delivering for Ballyboden. Very professional in his approach to the game, Keaney said he wouldn't come into the team unless he was fit and ready. He hadn't played hurling at that level for a while.

'So we agreed to put a programme together for him. He worked really hard in training. When he was satisfied that he was fit enough, we brought him into the squad. And he was a real asset for us.

'I felt for him in some ways, as he made the switch to the hurlers at just the wrong time from a football perspective. He was a brilliant footballer, and missed out on an All-Ireland title by just one year. But when he crossed over to hurling in 2011, he gave an immediate bounce to Anthony Daly's squad, and they won the National League.

'Danny Sutcliffe was another player who made his return in 2018. He was a top-class forward who had been an All Star in 2013.'

One issue going into that season was that the new management didn't have access to the Cuala players. They had won the 2017 All-Ireland club title, and after defending the Dublin Senior Championship were on route to another national crown.

That campaign would drag into late-March with the All-Ireland final going to a replay. There was no access to their inter-county players until after the National League.

'From our point of view, it wasn't an ideal set-up. But we knew that they were playing well at that level. They were training hard among themselves. We were watching their matches, and knew who was playing well. And I presume that the county players in their squad realised that they were going to be coming back into the Dublin team.

'Cuala winning two All-Irelands was a huge boost to Dublin hurling. And the injection of that winning mentality into the county squad naturally gave a real bounce to the group as a whole.

'The Cuala contingent's absence also gave us an opportunity to look at other guys.

'When we came in, confidence wasn't exactly sky high. They had endured a disappointing finish to 2017, losing to Tipperary 6-26 to 1-19.'

◄◄◆►►

CHRIS CRUMMEY

There was a lot of noise from outside… 'These lads don't have a hurling background!' But very quickly the lads just completely and utterly bought into Pat, Mickey and Anthony, and what they were trying to instil in the team.

A lot of what they were trying to do with the team was from a physical aspect. We probably weren't at the pitch of it the few years before that, from a physical and mental point of view. That was the first thing.

From a hurling point of view, players didn't have concerns at all. Pat and Mickey were very tuned in. Any concerns lads had really went away after the first few sessions when we saw the professional set-up they brought.

Mickey's character was brilliant. He was incredibly honest with the whole group. If you weren't putting it in or if he felt that you weren't getting the most out of yourself, he was just completely honest in telling you.

At that particular time with our group we really needed that. He was very tough with us, but he was brilliant.

He looked after the fitness work as well as the strength and conditioning.

Every type of fitness drill we did with Mickey was brilliant, as he always incorporated a bit of ball work in the drill. That was one of the key things he tried to get across to us... we're not here to be runners. We were there to hurl.

From the very start of the year, he told us exactly what he wanted from us. He set incredibly high standards. And if you didn't meet those standards, he would let you know about it fairly quickly.

He was also very hands-on. A lot of the drills he did were concentrated on stuff like our footwork, and body positions in tackles. There was real attention to detail. The small little bits... he really went into it.

He might have been 79 at the time, but he was pushing off lads, and wanted you to push by him. 'Attack this shoulder!' He'd want you to attack a weak shoulder. He was brilliant.

It probably did come as a bit of a shock to lads to see just how energetic he is. Doing drills with him... you'd nearly be reluctant to hit him a shoulder.

But he wanted you to!

He was so enthusiastic and energetic. And not just energetic for his age. He was energetic by anyone's standards.

He has a really positive personality.

He brought so much to us from that point of view, as well obviously as his knowledge and his experience from working over the years with teams.

He was mad! And great craic. He always has a joke.

CONAL KEANEY

I don't think there was any question I was going back, when I saw what [Pat Gilroy] was trying to do. He knew a lot of the players. He knew all the younger lads.

He knew his backroom team. This was months before it was announced he was taking over. So he had it all planned and he wanted me to be part of it. Sure why wouldn't you go for that?

He is very straight. To sort things out wasn't going to be that hard really if you had someone like him involved because he could say anything and lads would believe him. That was a great start.

And him bringing in Mickey Whelan as well was great… we knew what he would bring to it, honesty and working hard… and no bullshit.

◄◄◆▷►

DUBLIN GOT A few weeks' training under their belt in the autumn, before they went over to Boston for the Fenway Classic, a 'Super 11s' tournament. They took that seriously, and trained for it in the weeks leading up to the trip.

The management wanted to see every player available, and give them a chance to prove themselves. There were over 50 players in training initially, before a final squad was agreed upon.

The National League started with a heavy loss to Offaly in Croke Park, 2-25 to 1-15. It was a hammering, and a result that immediately piled on the pressure.

The defeat meant Dublin needed a result in the next match. They travelled away to Antrim in Corrigan Park, and edged it by the skin of their teeth, 0-23 to 0-22.

The win in Belfast, coupled with a final day victory over Laois, kept Dublin safely in Division 1B, and put them through to a quarter-final against Tipperary. Tipp pulled away in the second-half, which ended the springtime campaign.

Dublin then broke up for the April 'club month' before regrouping for the championship.

'While not many were giving us a chance, we were aiming high within the group. Some might have been surprised with our players' confidence when speaking in the media. But that was an important mindset which we drilled into them.

'It was a group perhaps lacking some confidence when we originally came in. We needed them to believe they could do it. We instilled that mentality. If they're not going out to win... *they're not going to win*. After a few more challenge matches, we were chomping at the bit, ready for championship.

'The opener was an opportunity to make a big statement, and that's exactly what we were looking to do. Kilkenny were coming to Parnell Park.'

IT WAS A match Dublin had been building towards, and they delivered. 'We played great, and were right there going down the home straight.'

Dublin were leading by a point in injury-time when corner-back Paddy Smyth was fouled coming out of defence. A free wasn't given, however, and Kilkenny got possession and scored the winning goal. It finished 1-24 to 3-16.

'It was a sucker punch. We were extremely unlucky to lose that game. But it showed we were well able to compete at that level.

'I spoke to both Brian Cody and Mick Dempsey at full-time. As we were walking off the pitch... both came over to us to shake hands.

'Cody told me, "We were lucky to get through this. You have a serious team there. If you keep playing like that, you're going to finish up in a good position".'

The new format that was introduced in 2018 meant that Dublin's Leinster campaign was far from over. They still had matches against Wexford, Offaly and Galway, with a real chance to progress.

'We instilled that in the players' mindsets. We had to go down to Wexford Park the following weekend and win.

'Wexford had an advantage as they had a 'bye week' in the first round. They were coming into the game fresh, while we were playing for the second weekend in succession.

'They opened up a big lead, but we came back at them late on.'

Dublin had a chance to equalise at the death, but didn't execute it correctly. Wexford went up the other end to seal a 0-22 to 2-14 win.

It was the same story. Dublin were coming close, but the win eluded them.

The following match was at home against Offaly in Parnell Park. Focus switched from qualifying for the All-Ireland series to avoiding relegation.

It was a must-win, against the team that had beaten Dublin well in the National League opener.

Dublin carried their form into that game, winning 2-24 to 0-13.

Going into the last game away to reigning All-Ireland champions Galway, Dublin were already eliminated. However, it was important to finish on a high. In similar fashion to the Kilkenny and Wexford defeats, they fell just short. Galway won 0-26 to 2-19.

'It was a disappointing end to the season, but it was only our first year. We felt we were moving in the right direction, and there would be a significant bounce in year two.

'Unfortunately, we never got a chance to build on what was a promising year. Pat was unable to continue, with added work commitments.

'It was tough to walk away from the project. We were working well with the group. But once he stepped down, that was that. Mattie Kenny got the job, after winning the two All-Ireland titles with Cuala. As is his right, he brought in his own backroom team.'

◄ ◄ ◆ ▷ ►

CHRIS CRUMMEY

We were working extremely hard during the springtime. We probably had a lot of training sessions right before National League games. We might not have been going into matches completely fresh.

From a players' point of view, we never talked about the championship in February or March. We always focused on each game, but in the big picture we were working hard in the early part of the year, in the weeks leading up to National League games that probably did have an impact on our performances.

We definitely improved as the league went on. There were new lads on the panel, and the management were trying different formations and different players. But we gathered a bit of momentum as it went on, and had a few wins by the end of it.

There was a bit of a turning point when we got the Cuala lads back. After winning an All-Ireland, they brought a freshness. We had a few challenge games against Limerick and Waterford in Parnell Park where we had good performances.

So there was confidence there that we were on the right track. We stepped it up significantly for the championship.

We played really well in the championship. But we were just lacking that bit of ruthlessness at the end of games. Maybe a bit of luck deserted us at times too.

From a performance point of view, it was chalk and cheese between the league and championship. From where we had come a few years previously, it was a massive, massive step up.

Pat, Mickey and Anthony brought their philosophy that we had to become very hard to beat. That year, we were very strong defensively. We only conceded one goal in the four championship games – the late one Kilkenny got in Parnell Park. That was a good stat to have... we were defensively sound.

They tried to make sure there were building blocks... that we would be defensively strong, hard to beat, and then we tried to develop it further.

Obviously lads were very disappointed at the time when Pat couldn't commit. You never want to go through one year of a management team and then it changes straight away. For any management coming in, it does take a bit of time and they have their own processes.

Definitely, you would have liked a continuous process at that time.

◄ ◄ ◆ ▷ ►

WHAT COULD PAT Gilroy, Mickey Whelan and Anthony Cunningham have achieved with three full years over that group?

'I think the players would have felt that we could have gone on to win an All-Ireland. Given the games we played in 2018 and the narrow scorelines, they would have felt confident.

'When some people talk about Dublin hurling, they write off the team because the likes of Ciarán Kilkenny and Con O'Callaghan have chosen football.

'But I still think there are more than enough hurlers in Dublin to win an All-Ireland title. The talent is undoubtedly there.

'We just need to get them in the right mould and get them to believe in themselves.'

Mickey and Pat Gilroy were back together on a Dublin sideline in 2017 when Pat took charge of the county hurlers (when they also asked the former Galway manager Anthony Cunningham to put his shoulder to the wheel).

They only had a year with the hurlers before Pat bowed out, but they did get to experience playing in Boston during the Fenway Classic.

It was not Mickey's first time to work with the county hurlers, as the great Lar Foley had asked him to be part of his management team in 1989.

« CHAPTER 14 »

HIS RETURN FROM the United States may have parked his association with soccer temporarily, but the sport was still to play a significant role in Mickey Whelan's life.

Soccer helped to facilitate his academic journey in America, but he also felt there was much to learn. It helped educate his coaching philosophies, and he was keen to learn more.

Upon his return to Ireland, Mickey enrolled with the FAI to gain his UEFA badges. He wanted to up-skill. He completed these over the course of a few years. There were both academic and practical elements to them.

'Joe McGrath, who was heavily involved with the FAI as the coaching director, helped me along my path. I think he respected what I was bringing to the table, in terms of my coaching philosophies and what I had learned in the U.S.

'He was somebody who worked hard for the FAI in those years. They were coming into a period where everyone was going to have to have qualifications to coach in soccer. So, he was setting up the whole thing with the FAI.'

◄ ◄ ◆ ▷ ►

'DUE TO MY gaelic football background, I was sometimes thought of as a *GAA man* in soccer circles.

'In 1990, I took a team over to the World Cup in Italy. It was a national colleges team, assembled from third level players from around Ireland.

'An unforgettable few weeks!

'We followed the Ireland team around the country, as 'Jack's Army' made it to the quarter-final of the World Cup. Wherever they would go… we would follow. And when we arrived in a new city, we would put out a message on the local radio station that this team of ours was looking to play matches against local sides.

'Attending the Republic of Ireland's matches was brilliant.

'After the penalty shoot-out win over Romania in the last 16, we all returned to our hotel in Genoa. We were all having a bite to eat, and I went up to my room for a shower.

'A few of our players had found out that the Ireland team was staying in a hotel just five minutes away. It was a gated complex, however. They walked up and were looking in, but they were not able to gain access so turned back towards our hotel.

'Bob Eustace, who was part of the management team on the trip, and I decided to walk up after the players. They were on the way back, and told us that there was no way of getting in. "I'm going up for a look anyway," I replied.

'They all turned and came along with us.

'When we got up to the gate, I saw the great sports journalist Con Houlihan inside.

'I also saw a former teammate of mine, Mick Byrne. Mick was on the Clanna Gael team alongside me when we won the Dublin senior title in 1968.'

Mick Byrne was Jack Charlton's right-hand man during those years. He worked with the Ireland team long before Charlton's arrival and long after his departure.

'MICK… MICK!' Mickey shouted over to him.

'Ah God, Mickey! Come in,' he replied. 'I can't… I have a big crowd with me.'

'Don't worry about that. Open the gates!'

They threw open the gates to let in the whole colleges team to mingle with the Ireland players.

'In we all went. And the first thing that happened was I ended up meeting the man of the moment Packie Bonner. He had just pulled off a save in the penalty shoot-out to send Ireland through to the World Cup quarter-final against Italy.'

'AFTERWARDS, JACK WAS letting all the players go out for a drink to celebrate, as they had a few days until their next match. And our panel joined them. I walked down into the town with the management team, who were going to find somewhere to sit down and have a drink.

'As I was walking down alongside Jack and his coaches, a police car was trailing us. They were worried about such a high-profile manager walking around in public like that. They were probably told they had to take care of him.

'But Jack didn't like the attention from the police. He turned to them… "Listen, there's no one going to shoot me. I'm going down to the ice-cream parlour to have a few pints and I'll be safe".

'As we were walking down, he turned to me. "Do you know where I'd rather be right now?"

'I was gobsmacked. Not only had he guided Ireland to a first ever World Cup, he had just led them into the quarter-finals!'

Mickey replied that he couldn't imagine Jack wanting to be anywhere else on earth!

'I'd love to be fishing on the river Moy!' said Jack.

'I looked around, expecting somebody to start laughing. But he was serious! We all sat down. Jack had a few pints. I was drinking lemonade and eating ice cream while chatting to him. We shot the breeze for the evening.

'A fascinating insight. He was a lovely man.

'I met him a few years later in 1996 again, at the ceremony in Limerick when he was awarded an honorary Irish citizenship… a real gentleman.'

◄◄◆►►

MICKEY WAS NO stranger to the road to Louth down through the years. He had managed the county's senior football team in the 80s, and had worked with a club side up there too.

But in 1994, he got involved with Dundalk FC.

He was brought in by Tommy Connolly.

Tommy and Mickey had crossed paths on the third level soccer circuit in Ireland, as he worked with Dundalk IT. Mickey also knew him through Louth GAA circles. They hit it off really well, and liked each other's ideas.

MICKEY WHELAN CHAPTER 14

Mickey had coached DIT against the Dundalk colleges team and he realised, *this guy knows his sport*. They became very good friends.

Mickey brought Tommy onto his coaching ticket over the Irish team at the World University Games.

At that time also, Tommy invited Mickey into Dundalk to work with some of the underage teams. It was an invitation he jumped at. He was more than happy to help out, and felt he could learn a thing or two along the way.

'I was working with players in the club. I was doing a bit of training with the underage, as well as the senior side. Tommy asked me to stay with the management team.'

Manager Turlough O'Connor left the club. And Dermot Keely, who had enjoyed a successful career in the League of Ireland as both a player and a manager, took the reins.

The day Dermot arrived, Mickey was doing a light warm-up with the team to get them ready for a match against Bohemians. Before he started the session, Dermot came over to him.

'Listen!' he said. 'I'm going to be bringing in my own guys with me. We won't be needing you!'

'Fine!' Mickey replied, understanding that new managers like to work with their own people usually.

Keely had just left the role as manager of Longford Town, and had his own ideas. He had a coach with whom he worked with in Longford, who was going to join him in Dundalk.

Mickey began to pack his stuff before heading home.

'No!' Keely said. 'Could you do the session today anyway?'

'No problem.'

So Mickey did the training with the team. When he was done, he began to head away. A minute later, he heard a shout.

'Hey! Mickey!'

He looked around, and there was Dermot Keely running after him!

'Come here, Mickey!' he said. 'You did a great job in training, and the players think you should stay. I didn't know you could do this kind of stuff. I didn't expect they would be so happy with you. Would you be willing to stay?'

'What about your buddy coming from Longford?' Mickey asked.

185

'I'll sort that. I want you to come back.'

'No. You can think about it!' Mickey replied.

'I'm not thinking about it. This is it… you're staying here with me!'

Mickey was strapped in for the season.

AT THE BEGINNING of the 1994-95 League of Ireland season, Dundalk FC were battling some financial difficulties. It was not the first nor last such instance in the league.

'As a management team, we just kept the players focused on the football. That's all we could control. As long as they received their payments on time, they were happy to keep their heads down.

'The League of Ireland is a marathon, not a sprint. It is a long slog over the course of a season. In that regard, fitness was going to be key.

'We put in a tough pre-season that year to build up a core level of fitness. After that, it was all about simply maintaining those levels. They did very heavy, strong pre-season training. I did that with Dublin teams too. You can build their fitness in the pre-season, and then simply keep it at a level. If you had a week without a game, you could put a hard session in here or there to bring them back up.

'But the first few weeks of pre-season are all about putting money in the bank, upon which you can draw throughout the year. The Dundalk players liked the work I was doing with them. It was different to running laps all the time.

'The running we did was short-distance speed work. I was then getting them to work with the ball. They were used to a pre-season where it was all heavy training. We would do two hard sessions a week, and take it easy on the third day. It was important to let them recover too.

'We put in a strong body of work over the six weeks. The first half of that was running up hills, getting them back into the flow of things. Then I introduced more ball work. Back then, if you weren't running the stuffing out of them, people might have thought there was something wrong with you!

'But we had a good group, and they were happy to buy into what I was bringing. There were some great players on that team, stalwarts in the league like Brian Byrne, Joe Hanrahan and Tom McNulty.

◄ ◄ ◆ ► ►

TOM MCNULTY

Mickey had a fabulous reputation from the GAA. I didn't know him personally, but I knew of him. I knew he had been very successful at gaelic football.

He had played for Dublin… managed St Vincent's. So everyone was well aware of what he did.

But we had not seen him working in soccer.

What I noticed with Mickey was, firstly, he was very intelligent. He was strict. He was a straight-talker. He was a great coach. And a great motivator.

The motivating factor was his number one. Dermot had a habit of roaring and shouting at people. Mickey was great at coming along after Dermot put somebody down, and lifting them back.

I was about 34 or 35 at that stage. I was kind of thinking… Am I coming to the end of my career?

Half-way through pre-season, I just felt absolutely knackered.

And Mickey said, 'You just have to keep going… there's only another week of pre-season and then it will be behind you'.

He was very cute in how he went about things. I think the transformation from gaelic football to soccer… not many have done it like him, if any.

I'd say we were the oldest team ever to win a league, but also one of the fittest teams. And I think that is a great testament to Mickey's coaching. We were disciplined, we were fit, and we had a great belief. And that was instilled every time we had a training session.

The training sessions became more intense. The passing was getting better, it was getting quicker. Your recovery was getting better… quicker. It was all a testament to what we were doing in training, and it started transforming our play on the pitch.

Some of the sessions Mickey laid out were completely different to what we'd been doing.

I remember one drill. It was a session of pure football. Replicating all the different runs you'd be doing in a game. Some of it was with the ball… some of it was without the ball. But it was all very intense.

He had all these grids laid out, and people were thinking… Jesus, what are we doing?

But when we got into it, it was really, really intense.

So, one grid you could be heading the ball. But you weren't just heading it, you could be heading it to score a goal... then into the next grid where you are heading a cross. And then you were into the next grid where you were doing short runs, closing people down.

It was all bang-bang-bang.

There were no breaks in between.

The session lasted for I'd say about 40 minutes. And in that 40 minutes, you had done all the running that you'd do in a match in 90 minutes. You were heading the ball, you were chesting the ball, you were closing people down.

So I asked him after that session, 'Mickey, where in the name of God did you come up with that?'

And he said, 'Well I was thinking about it for a long time, Tommy and I didn't know whether it would work.'

These were all experienced players. We all thought... Jesus, that was a great session!

Everyone was tired. You were getting that touch of the ball every few seconds. You were getting your runs in. It was all match situations.

So you were running to close somebody down on the ball quickly. And then you were away into another drill. And then the fella who was on the ball was away into another drill. And somebody else was in his place. It was like clockwork. After about... I'd say about six weeks of that, you could certainly see the team getting fitter and all coming together.

JOE HANRAHAN

During the winter months many teams are just running up and down the field for fitness. As a coach, Mickey Whelan had us using the ball constantly no matter how much running we were doing. His techniques were great at killing two birds with one stone like that.

We worked on our physical fitness and our skills at the same time.

◄ ◄ ◆ ► ►

IT WAS A rollercoaster season.

'The atmosphere at games at Oriel Park was brilliant. We were by no means favourites for the league at the start, and weren't listed amongst the front-runners.

'But what we did have was an experienced squad, with players willing to put in the hard yards.'

Dundalk got off to a poor start, however, failing to win any of their first three games. Derry City and Shelbourne were the pace-setters.

'Dermot is a great guy. Completely mad! But a great man.

'He was great at managing. He would assemble the squad and pick the starting 11. But he left the coaching side of things to Tommy and myself. He knew where his strengths were, and relied on us to coach.

'As the season progressed, we began to gather momentum. We were breathing down the neck of the league leaders, and picking up narrow wins.'

As the campaign began to turn towards the home straight, Keely turned to Mickey and suggested that they ramp up the training intensity. 'We can't afford to slump. We need these guys to be as fit as possible,' he stressed.

Mickey disagreed.

'No, the other guys are going to do that,' Mickey explained. 'We've done a very, very tough pre-season. We're just maintaining that now.

'The other teams are going to be saying, "We have to do more". But we need to do less hard work… and more games and ball work.'

Dermot put his hands on his head! 'Okay, but if we don't win this league, you'll be responsible!'

Mickey has always been a big believer in rest periods. There is a time for hard work, but there is also a time to take it easy.

It is important to retain players' energy reserves, and also to prevent injury.

'They bought into it very quickly as players. They saw what I was doing and they were feeling great. And instead of hard running when the season got underway, I was using the ball. It was all about sprinting and ball work. We were building fitness in the game situations and they loved that.

'When Dermot suggested an increased training load, I told him we should decrease it. I knew the dangers of the players burning out after a long season.

'He told me in no uncertain terms that it would be on my head if we didn't win that league!'

◄◄◆►►

TOM MCNULTY

I remember training one night for an hour, and Mickey came along and said, 'Right Tom, that's you done for the night… in you go!'

Dermot was up in arms! 'What are we doing?'

'Look, he's one of our main players!' Mickey told him. 'You need him to have all of his energy levels for the match at the weekend. You can't leave everything here on the training ground.'

That was Mickey's argument.

We weren't young players. We were old players. So the training sessions, when it came to the time of the season where you're either going to fall or you're going to kick on… it was just a matter of ticking over.

We wanted to leave everything for matchday.

Dermot had never worked with Mickey before that year. When Mickey came in, it was funny to see the two of them interact, because Mickey is very strong-willed… and Dermot is very strong-willed.

To hear Mickey tell Dermot that he hadn't got a clue was funny at times!

The amount of games we won that season with late goals was unbelievable.

We scored the least amount of goals of the top eight teams, but we conceded just 25 in 33 matches.

That was a lot of the work that Mickey and Tommy had done on the defensive side of the game and also on our fitness. We were out-lasting teams.

His communication skills on the training ground were something else. It was new for me. Something different.

During training matches, he would see small things that would make a huge difference to your game.

Maybe just saying… 'You're giving the ball too quick… just take your time!' Another time, maybe he told people to give it a bit quicker. 'You keep going left all the time. Instead of going left… go right!'

It was just the small things. He was very good at getting his point across to you. And when you needed a bollocking… you got a bollocking! We were all experienced players, it was very seldom that we needed a bollocking.

But when we needed it, we got it. He wasn't slow to tell somebody off.

As a coach, to come from gaelic to soccer and on the first attempt to get a team to win a league that we had no chance of winning, it's a great testament to him as a coach.

It got to a point in the season where Mickey, Tommy and Dermot started talking about winning the league. And that was all they were talking about. They drilled it into everybody… 'We have a chance now. We are going to win the league!'

We just kept nicking a result… nicking a result… nicking a result. And we were on the coat-tails of the leaders all the time. But it was the last six weeks, the business end of it, where all of our hard work through the year started to come to fruition.

We were together as a team. The coaches were together as a group.

They were all focused. They all knew the mindset… This is what we need to do. We need to push on to another level.

We got 15 points from the last six games. Three of those five wins were on a 1-0 scoreline. So we had a great belief as a group. The coaches had a great belief.

Mickey can certainly be proud of what we achieved that year.

TOMMY CONNOLLY

We finished stronger than any team in the league that year. When others began to tire, we were actually getting stronger.

Mickey's training kept the team peaking again and again throughout the campaign. He'd measured out exactly what the team would need and he was proved right.

◄◄◆►►

DUNDALK WERE FEROCIOUSLY chasing Derry City and Shelbourne, reeling them in slowly, but surely. It all came down to the final day of the season.

Dundalk were hosting Galway United, but needed other results to go their way.

They were level with Shelbourne on points, but Derry were one ahead.

Fortune smiled on Dundalk that day. Athlone Town held Derry to a draw. Shelbourne could also only manage a point against St Patrick's Athletic.

That opened the door. Goals from Tom and Mick Doohan sealed a 2-0 win, for a dramatic and unlikely league title.

'As I was taking on the Dublin job at the end of 1995, I had to step away from Dundalk after one season. But what a season. A hugely enjoyable year.

'We had a brilliant time together that year.

'Dermot lives out in Spain now, running a pub. When all of this coronavirus stuff is over and travel is possible again, I'm going to see him one more time.'

Out in Italy with the Irish Universities team, Mickey got to spend the day with Jack Charlton after Ireland qualified for the 1990 World Cup quarter-finals (and here he is with Jack some years later at a coaching event).

Dermot Keely (right) asked Mickey to help guide Dundalk to the league title in 1995 (here's captain James Coll with the trophy at a homecoming in Oriel Park). It was a brilliant and exciting year in Mickey's coaching life.

« CHAPTER 15 »

COACHING DUNDALK WAS not Mickey's first time working in Louth. It's a county in which he has spent several years on the sideline through various codes.

Following Dublin's 1985 All-Ireland final loss to Kerry, Kevin Heffernan stepped aside as manager of the county's senior football team for a second time.

After the massive success he had enjoyed, there were big boots to fill.

Mickey Whelan's name was brought up as a potential successor. A few months prior to that, he had guided St Vincent's to the All-Ireland Club Championship final which was lost to Castleisland Desmonds.

Given how close he was with Kevin, however, he did not want to be the one taking the reins. Speculation was growing in the media, when he was contacted by Louth GAA. Louth were looking for a new senior football manager. 'It was an exciting proposition in its own right, but it also presented an opportunity for me to remove my name from the Dublin reckoning.

'It was the right decision for me at the time.

'Louth were always a dangerous prospect going back to my own playing days, and I was looking to get them firing on all cylinders. All-Ireland titles might not always be the goal for teams, but we felt there was progress to be made. I was asked to improve them, and that's what I tried to do.

'I brought Danny Nugent, Jim Thornton and Danny Culligan into my backroom team... three Louth guys. I was an *outside* manager coming into the county, so it was important to have locals by my side, guys who knew the landscape inside-out.'

Outside managers were not as common back then.

Mickey was aware that there might have been an element of opposition against his appointment; a Dub coming into the county to take the reins.

'That prejudice was never a problem when we were winning, but if something was going wrong, there were moans coming from certain quarters.

'If you lost a game narrowly in the National League, it was not the be-all and end-all. We were building towards the Leinster Championship. I was designing a game-plan and working on the team. But some people would use that as a stick with which to beat us.

'I was training the team hard in order to peak for the summer months.'

◄ ◄ ◆ ▷ ►

DAVID REILLY
(FORMER LOUTH FOOTBALLER)

Football was at a low ebb in Louth when Mickey came in.

Jimmy Mulroy was manager when I first came into the squad in 1984, after they pushed Dublin close the previous year.

They went then for a five-man selection committee in 1985. They picked a lot of the older characters that were synonymous with Louth's successful time in the 50s. The county went backwards. They were all good footballing men, but they had sort of lost touch. At that stage, it was more than just picking a team. It was about communicating, getting to know guys and seeing what makes those fellas tick.

We got hockeyed in the championship of 1985 against Offaly down there. It was an embarrassing scoreline. After that, the Louth County Board decided to go for an outside manager. Mickey's coaching methods were a huge culture shock for a number of older players in the set-up. The mentality at the time was that your strength and conditioning came from laps, sit-ups and push-ups… and maybe putting a fella on your back and running shuttles. But Mickey changed all of that.

Everything was done with the ball, especially all the running. Once guys got up and running they could see the benefit. Everything was sharp.

He expected us all to be fit and able to run anyway. He was taking that as a given.

Maybe that's why he went with so many young guys in the squad. They could cover the ground. They were athletic. They were up and down the field, so it was just a case of improving their skill-set and their ability to make the right decisions.

At the time, a lot of gaelic football was when fellas got the ball, it was about how far they could kick it. Mickey was one of the first guys to say, 'Why kick it away? That means you have to work hard to get it back again'.

Dundalk CBS had won a Leinster Colleges Championship that year, and Mickey pulled in guys from there and also from the minor team. Players like Stefan White, John Osbourne, Gerry Curran and Seamus O'Hanlon all came through around that time.

So he brought in a whole new wave of young lads.

They were all big, athletic and strong.

It was a big panel. Anyone that was making excuses, or fellas that were relying on reputations were in trouble. He went with his own team, and he built from there.

There was a great buzz around the county at that time, and Mickey gave us a serious bounce straight away after coming in. He surrounded himself with good football people in Louth. Danny Nugent, Danny Culligan and Jim Thornton had all only finished up, they were still playing club football. They were people the players could associate with... could see in the flesh having played against them in club games.

Mickey was a great man for thinking outside the box.

People would stereotype you, and say you were this type of player or that type of player. He was able to see different qualities in different people.

I remember he put Martin McCann, who was a wing-forward on the previous teams, at centre half-back. Martin established himself there, and you couldn't move him from that position then!

◄◄◆►►

'I GOT THE job in late-1985, and immediately went to work. I attended several of the matches in the club championship, looking to scour the county for talent. I was trying to keep the head down at these games, and hoped not to get spotted.

'It was not public knowledge at that stage that I had been appointed.

'The appetite for football in the county was clear, even though it is often considered a soccer stronghold. There were 5,000 packed in for the county final in 1985.'

In that game, Clan na Gael overcame Roche Emmets, 1-6 to 0-4.

The match was settled by a goal from a 16-year-old, one of the brightest prospects about. Steve Staunton rifled a left-footed shot into the net. He looked a cracking corner-forward.

Mickey was looking forward to getting him into the Louth panel.

A bit more digging, however, informed him that Staunton, a student at the DLS in Dundalk, was already making a name for himself on soccer fields.

Unfortunately, from a Louth GAA perspective, his exploits with Dundalk FC were getting him noticed by English clubs. And he moved over to Liverpool the following year.

'What a gaelic footballer he would have been! I worked with his brother a few years later when I coached Clan na Gael.

'Nonetheless, we had fruitful preparations ahead of the National League. I trained the team no differently to any other side I had coached. Everything was with the ball, challenging them to improve their decision-making among other elements.'

At that time, the National League divisions were all linked. Four teams from Division 1, two sides from Division 2 and one county from each of the two eight team Division 3 groups qualified for the quarter-finals.

Louth were in Division 3, and enjoyed a positive campaign. From seven matches, they picked up five wins. It was not enough to reach the knockout stages unfortunately, as they finished second in their group behind Derry.

It left the team in good shape ahead of the championship opener, when they beat Longford convincingly, 2-11 to 1-5 in Drogheda. It was a brilliant atmosphere, with 5,000 fans in attendance.

◄◄◆►►

1986 LEINSTER SFC FIRST ROUND
LOUTH 2-11 LONGFORD 1-15

Louth will step out for their next Leinster Senior Football Championship clash against Offaly with a certain amount going for them under new manager and former Dublin footballer, Mickey Whelan.

That game will also be at Drogheda, where yesterday this Louth side beat Longford and showed that their 10 victories from 11 previous outings, which included challenge games, were not 'fluke' results. They showed a character which saw them playing much more impressively against the wind in the second-half, when the spectators had almost made up their minds that the game from then on was going to belong to Longford, who faced the strong wind in the first-half.

Though they enjoyed so much of the play in the second-half against the wind, will they be allowed to dominate to such an extent against Offaly? Only then will we get the answer to whether or not Louth are on the way back.

It is 1957 since they last won the Leinster title. But I have a feeling that if they get a few things right, such as taking points when they are on – and they missed many with the wind at their backs in the first-half yesterday – then manager Whelan may have something to look forward to in the months ahead.

◄◄◆►►

OFFALY HAD WON the 1982 All-Ireland title and were still a force to be reckoned with. They had hammered Louth in the championship the previous year, 3-16 to 1-8. There was another full house in Drogheda.

Louth played some fine football, but came up agonisingly short. Offaly won by two points, 1-13 to 2-8, but the home supporters felt they were denied a stonewall penalty late in the game. Had it been given, Louth might have been through to a semi-final against Dublin.

◄◄◆►►

DAVID REILLY

There was a definite penalty.

Johnny McDonnell was pulled down. The sports pages at the time showed pictures of him going through and being dragged back by the jersey! But the referee waved it on. And that's when the game was in the melting pot.

We ended up losing the game by two points. At that stage, there was a bit of a buzz around the county after we had beaten Longford in the first game.

◄◄◆►►

ON THE WHOLE, it was a year of real progress.

Mickey felt the county was moving in the right direction.

The next season followed a similar trajectory. Louth held their own in the National League, but once more missed out on the knockout stages. Galway qualified for the quarter-finals from their group, as Louth finished with three wins and a draw from seven matches. That led into the championship, where Longford were first up in the first round once more. This time it was in Longford's backyard, but Louth came through with a similar result.

◄◄◆►►

1987 LEINSTER SFC FIRST ROUND
LONGFORD 0-8 LOUTH 0-13

Three players were sent off in a free-ridden Leinster SFC game at Pearse Park, Longford, as Louth overcame the home side more easily than the scoreline suggests.

Before a huge home following in a crowd of about 5,000, Longford started in great style and had three points on the board in four minutes. Louth then took complete control and after their first point after six minutes, they never looked back and led by 0-7 to 0-4 at the interval. Longford's collapse continued and Louth went seven points clear 15 minutes into the second-half with Seamus O'Hanlon, John McDonnell and Richard Culhane doing most of the damage.

Despite kicking an alarming number of wides, Louth were always the better side, with O'Hanlon and the roving McDonnell causing all sorts of problems for the defence.

1987 LEINSTER SFC QUARTER-FINAL
WICKLOW 1-7 LOUTH 0-8

A punched goal by full-forward Richie Griffin from a shot by Pat Baker gave Wicklow a narrow two-points win over Louth in their Leinster Championship quarter-final at Aughrim. The goal came just eight minutes from the end and at the right psychological moment for Wicklow, as Louth had just drawn level for the second time in the previous minute.

◄◄◆►►

LOSING TO WICKLOW was a hammer blow.

There was grumbling in the local media.

'It was a pity, because I was enjoying my time there,' Mickey recalls. 'But I was not going to put up with it. It just was not worth the hassle. I didn't want that rubbish.'

◄◄◆▷►

DAVID REILLY

We went down to Wicklow and got completely hijacked altogether down in Aughrim. We were hot, hot favourites. I don't know whether it was just people buying into the whole perception of just having to turn up on the day?

But that's what happened. We were beaten, 1-7 to 0-8.

Mickey definitely left Louth football in a better place than where he found it. When he left Louth football the structures in place were much more professional. Bits like food after training, access to physios, people getting medical care.

PETER BRANNIGAN
(FORMER LOUTH COUNTY BOARD CHAIRMAN)

He came down to help out my club Clan na Gael in Dundalk, and he played a major role in helping us to win the county championship.

He knows football inside out.

At the time he left Louth, there may have been a feeling among people that an outside manager wasn't needed to manage the county team.

It was a pity, because Mickey has a lot to offer.

◄◄◆▷►

STEPPING AWAY FROM the Louth job severed his ties with the county for a few years.

That was, until 1992 when Mickey Heeney gave Mickey a call. Heeney was managing Clan na Gael, who had lost three county finals in the previous four years.

They were looking for the final piece to their jigsaw, and Mickey was invited into the camp. 'He had a brilliant grip of the game, a really bright guy. I'd have a brilliant relationship with him, and we're still in touch.

'The team were there or thereabouts, but they needed the belief to get over the line. That is what had let them down in previous finals.

'We reached the county final and were up against Dundalk Gaels. Being honest, we were blessed to escape with a draw. Before the replay, I decided we needed to change up the team. They weren't happy when I had a cut at them.

'There were some young players I brought into the fold. And I switched things up positionally too. I moved some of the forwards back to the half-back line.

'Some of the players were moaning, especially those who had dropped out of the team. But also those pulled out of position. I asked them, "Which is the best team you have seen?"

'Kerry was the obvious reply they gave me.

'I told them, if they went through each of the Kerry players… nearly every one of them played in different positions at different stages… be it half-back, midfield or in the forwards.

'They might have been midfielders or forwards for their club, but Mick O'Dwyer would put them in different spots on the county team.

'I made the point to them, and underlined that we needed the belief. That was crucial. You need courage to get over the line in county finals. They had the talent, but had to get it right mentally.'

Clan na Gael won the replay well, hammering Dundalk Gaels 3-11 to 1-6. 'I was delighted for them. They clearly had the potential; it was about going out there and delivering.

'There were celebrations late into the night.'

Irish soccer legend Steve Staunton was someone Mickey could have used when he took charge of Louth in the mid-80s, but he had to park his gaelic football career. Seamus O'Hanlon and Stefan White were two of the excellent players he got to work with.

« CHAPTER 16 »

WHEN MICKEY CAME home from America in 1975, he finished off his Masters degree from West Virginia University. He still had research and study to complete in Dublin.

He was working in Killester Vocational School on Collins Avenue, but offers were still coming from a variety of universities in the United States to return. Davis and Elkins asked him to go back to pursue his studies and work in their soccer programme. In 1978, he decided to go for it.

He accepted the job, handed in his notice to William Purcell in Killester, and paid for the flights. He was all set to leave.

Irene was going to be staying in Dublin with the kids.

THE NIGHT BEFORE his flight, all the bad memories of the last time he emigrated suddenly came flooding back. He remembered the tears shed as he was leaving. Mickey was crying and Irene was crying.

'Tearing myself apart from her almost broke me.

'I was not able to do it again.

'I decided not to go.'

He let Davis and Elkins know that he would not be taking the job. He went back to William Purcell and told him that he would be staying in Ireland. William was happy to hear that news.

Mickey had submitted an official letter, informing the school of his departure. The Department of Education convened once a month to go through any staff changes, but they had not held a meeting since Mickey had issued his notice, so nothing was processed.

'Sit down there Michael for a minute!' William picked up the phone in his office to ring the department.

'I sent you a letter that said Michael Whelan had stepped down. Has that gone to the committee yet?'

'No that won't be for another two weeks,' came the reply.

'Send it back! I've talked him into staying!'

Working primarily as a PE teacher in Killester was an enjoyable and fulfilling time. Helping teenagers develop athletically enabled Mickey to put his studies into practice. But he was still hungry to learn more. The natural academic progression following his Masters degree was to undertake a PhD. He promised himself that it was something he would undertake at some point down the line.

He spent 10 memorable years at Killester Vocational School.

In 1984, however, he was offered a position in Dublin Institute of Technology on Bolton Street. The attraction was clear. He was raising a young family, and there was a significant pay rise.

In 1975, he had started on the lowest rung of the teaching ladder, and it would take time to climb the incremental pay scale.

DIT offered him a chance to fast track what would have been 10 years working as a teacher at Killester Vocational School. It was a no-brainer.

Having spent time in third-level education in America, Mickey was now returning to it here in Ireland.

'This was a role purely focused on physical education and sports science. It enabled me to develop my own knowledge, and I stayed there for the remainder of my full-time working life… right up until my retirement in 2004.'

Complete retirement would never have suited Mickey, however.

He continued lecturing in Dublin City University after the sports department there asked him to take on a part-time role.

It was a job that suited him. DCU was the local university, and he ended up working with their Sigerson Cup team.

Finally, he also felt the time was right to undertake his PhD.

'I APPROACHED DR Niall Moyna with my concept, and he was fully supportive.

'Niall and I developed a close working relationship over the years. I studied my PhD under his guidance, and I brought him into the coaching teams with St Vincent's and Dublin.

'He was enthusiastic the second I discussed the notion of my PhD. He told me to go for it.

'It was a topic in which I fully believed. In fact, I already knew the results. But I needed to scientifically prove it to hammer the point home.

'Down through the years, I always knew that small-sided games are the way forward at underage levels.

'Playing 15-a-side matches on big pitches for players at under-12 and under-14 was always the status quo. But it was madness.

'If you reduced the size of the playing field proportionately in line with the decreased number of players, everybody would be far more involved.

'When an under-12 game is 15-a-side, a small group of the most developed players dominate at midfield, centre-forward and centre-back. Meanwhile, the corner-backs and corner-forwards might only get one or two touches each in the entire match.

'They are simply standing there, getting cold. They might be having a chat with their pals. Twiddling their thumbs.

'If you reduce it to five-a-side or seven-a-side on smaller pitches, there is none of that whatsoever. Everybody is involved... running, catching, kicking. End-to-end stuff.

'The action is never far away.

'It was clear as day to me. But in order to lend gravitas to my theory and positively affect change in underage sport throughout Ireland, I needed to offer scientific evidence.

'Along with Niall, I came up with the title. And it did not change from day one until its publication in 2011:

Effect of altering the number of players, the dimensions of the playing area and the playing rules on the number of selected technical skills performed, possession characteristics, physiological responses and levels of enjoyment and perceived competence during gaelic football in prepubescent and adolescent boys.

FROM THE BEGINNING, it did exactly what it said on the tin.

However, titling it was one thing. Proving it was another.

Now it was time for the hard work.

First of all, Mickey had to recruit participants for the studies.

'We gathered a group of young footballers to take part over the course of a year. I had to get written permission from each of their parents, and they would assemble each week to play games of football.

'Along with undergraduates and Masters students who were helping me with the project, we would stage the tests.

'Each child was fitted with a GPS and heart monitor to track movement and activity levels.'

Some weeks they would play 15-a-side matches.

Other weeks it would be five-a-side, seven-a-side or nine-a-side.

'We would video each of the games to review afterwards. I spent long days and nights over the following two years, reviewing the tapes. I would have to watch a match back each time for every player. I would collect data on the number of times he would be in possession, his kicks, hand-passes, hops, solos, drops, tackles… you name it.

'It was painstaking, but worthwhile.

'Once you are making progress, you can do it. The students who were working alongside me were a massive help too. And some of that work went towards their degrees.

'I have never believed in shortcuts. In every facet of my life, if I do something, I'm going to do it right the whole way from the beginning. My father taught me that from a young age… you either do something right or you don't do it at all.

'After each match on the day, we would also survey the children. They would be separated, and each of my helpers would ask them to score their enjoyment of the match on a scale of one to five. One was *not at all*… and five was *very much*.

'Small-sided games out-performed the 15-a-side matches across the board. It was night and day.

'The smaller the numbers that were involved, the more enjoyment levels went up. The number of catches, passes, kicks, scoring attempts, pick-ups, blocks, interceptions, hops, solos and touches all increased exponentially the more you decreased the numbers of players on a field.

'The results screamed out from the page.

'I submitted my findings in 2011 and my PhD was published.

'The findings were clear: *The overall results indicate that for young players, small sided games are more appropriate than the adult 15-a-side game format to learn and develop the technical and tactical skills of gaelic football in an enjoyable environment, while also experiencing a physiological stimulus appropriate to their maturational stage.'*

'DESPITE THE PhD, I never call myself Dr Mickey Whelan, unless in academic settings. If I am presenting at a conference or attending anything in an academic setting, I will use the title to recognise DCU.

'But it is not something I use day-to-day.

'Around that time, Pat Daly, the GAA's Director of Games Development and Research, was investigating the benefits of small-sided games for underage gaelic football and hurling. It was perfect timing.

'Here I was undertaking scientific research on the very matter. I had an avalanche of evidence to prove that this was the way forward with gaelic football.'

Mickey's research was gratefully received in Croke Park.

It helped to lay the foundations for 'Go Games', which are now commonplace in every GAA club around Ireland.

'The fact that my findings were implemented so quickly by the GAA is a huge source of pride. It did not just end up on a bookshelf gathering dust.

'It is freely available online. I often have people getting in touch to congratulate me, or comment on how it was ahead of its time.'

'FROM MY PERSPECTIVE, winning should not be important in sport until the ages of 15 or 16.

'Before that, if you have a group of 30 or 40 young players, split them into smaller groups and play a few different seven-a-side matches or something along those lines. If there are four coaches there, play four 'five vs five' games, or two 'four vs fours' if numbers dictate.

'Play 10 or 12 minutes… then switch the teams, so they're not always playing against the same team. All the time they're coming up against different players… taller players, smaller players… and they're acquiring the nuances of how to get around their opponents.

'Instead of drills, drills… drills, where they are thinking… *What did Mickey say to me? What does he want me to do?* Let them off…

'Let them play.

'Let them make mistakes.

'Let them learn.

'When you see youngsters coming off a field, they are all joking and laughing. They will forget about the result quickly enough.

'The danger of hammering home the importance of winning too early is stark.

'If winning is everything to a coach and a team at that age, there will be small guys on the sideline that are never going to get a chance. Playing the best players will give you the best chance of winning, but that will cause long-term damage. Drop-out rates will rise. And it is not always the best players at under-12 who will be the best players in that group at under-18 or older.

'If you focus on the big guys who are half a stone heavier than anyone else on the field, they will walk through at under-8, under-9… under-10. But at 15 or 16, they might have a growth spurt which can mess with their centre of balance. It can take time to adapt to your new size. And coaches can't understand why those players are not delivering. They might lose patience.

'Sometimes, it is the small corner-forward at under-12 who turns out to be the best senior player. People develop at different speeds. But that peripheral player at underage is not going to hang around until the senior grade if he does not get game-time. If he is left on the sideline twiddling his thumbs because a coach values winning over development, he will soon get fed up and quit the sport.'

'KIDS JUST WANT to play competitive and enjoyable matches.

'Look out on the street if there are young children playing a game of football unsupervised. If it becomes too one-sided, they will look to level the playing field. If one team is winning 10-0, they will stop the game and swap the teams around to balance it up.

'They do that themselves!

'So how can a coach on the sideline know any better?

'Teachers or managers who want to win at all costs won't let smaller guys play. They will stick with the big guys all the time.

'Running the pitch does not do the bigger guys any good in the long-term.

They are not reading games. They are not learning how to get a pass and take one.

'By letting everyone play, and adding impediments such as a minimum number of passes needed before shooting, they are learning all the time, unknown to themselves.

'Let the kids play.

'That is my mantra. All of them.

'Right up until the age of 14 or 15, it is not about winning. It is about playing. Parents or coaches roaring on a sideline are ridiculous.

'They are shaming their kids and they are harming everyone else.

'If I was in charge of an underage team that had ultra-competitive parents, I would have a chat with them, meet them all. "I'm going to make them better players in the long run, and everyone is going to play. I want them to grow, I want to help them develop, but I don't want anyone coming in onto the pitch. Will you accept that?"

'A couple of them might go off in a huff, disagreeing with you.

'But when they see all the other parents behaving themselves and not shouting, maybe clapping when the game is over, they will understand.'

'WHEN I WAS doing the tests with the youngsters for the PhD, not one mother or father was roaring at the players during the games. They were just admiring all the kids enjoying themselves, getting the chance to play well or do something good. It was just natural.

'Players go down to the GAA club to play football and hurling. They do not go there to do drills. The coaches are simply there to facilitate the players.

'It is like a pianist. If you want to play the piano, *you have to play the piano*. You can spend all the time studying sheet music and theory, but you will improve the most when you sit down and tickle the ivory.

'Eventually, you get so good that you do not have to look down to see where your fingers are. You just play.

'You are on autopilot.

'To extend that analogy to sport, you have to play gaelic football to improve at gaelic football. Create game-based situations in training. Games bring you on more than drills.

'And in fitness, you have to train with the ball or create similar running drills to replicate the runs you would make in a match.

'I never got a team to run laps.

'They are gaelic footballers… not cross-country runners!

'But for underage players, they go down to the field with their pals to play football. Let them play football.'

◄ ◄ ◆ ▷ ►

NIALL MOYNA

I had a position in DCU around the time Mickey was retiring from DIT. He came in, and we got to know each other.

He always had this tremendous interest in education and in bettering himself. And it wasn't so much about getting a PhD. He just wanted more knowledge. He had this hunger for knowledge. It wasn't for affirmation. Mickey is not into that sort of stuff at all. He never wants to stop learning.

Around 2005, we then decided that he would pursue a PhD. He had told me about this idea all his life. He had this belief that the game should be your teacher. He felt we were coaching skills out of players.

We were losing what people learned on the street and the playground, because we were sanitising coaching and he was very worried about that.

He believed that allowing people to learn the game through playing, was a much more effective way.

It had been in his head for years. He knew he was right.

He just needed to prove it to everyone else. It was something he had believed for years and years. But every time you do a piece of research, you have to have a hypothesis to drive it.

For a PhD, you have to have a hypothesis. Most students do it through reading literature, and then they come up and they generate one.

Mickey had it through living and experience.

And all it was, it was confirming everything that he said. And all his hypotheses all came through, exactly as he had expected.

I had spent time in America. Upon my return to Ireland, I was concerned about seeing how the sport had moved from a very amateur game to a professional one. But not just at the higher level... these things about development squads and selecting players, it really worried me.

Along with Noel McCaffrey, we organised what we called, 'Open games' at DCU every Saturday morning. We invited youngsters from maybe 15-to-20 clubs around Dublin – all the way over as far as Kilmacud – to join in.

The one proviso was that every child that came that morning would get to play. We didn't care what their talent was, or how good or how bad they were. The whole idea was to be inclusive.

It was challenging for us... we got the coaches to give us a rough idea who were the good players and who were the weak ones.

We used this as the sample for much of Mickey's PhD research. Our undergraduate students would help out.

Within three weeks of this, a parent came to me and said, 'You have no idea how transformative this has been in my child's life'. The child woke him up at 5am to make sure they weren't late for DCU at 10am. For the first time in his life, he was getting to play!

There was something there, and Mickey was obviously heavily involved in it. So we met with Pat Daly in Croke Park.

And we explained to Pat about this whole notion of affording every youngster an opportunity. The GAA was meant to be a social organisation, affording every child the opportunity to play. And that was the genesis of the Go Games.

We agreed with Pat that Mickey would do the PhD. His hypothesis was that taking this game-based approach would give every child the opportunity. Mickey then got funding through the GAA to undertake his PhD.

You could structure the games in such a way that it's a learning environment for them. I'm a physiologist, I wanted to add physiology into it as well. We looked at the physiological response to the small-sided games, and how it affected them. Did they feel more competent playing the small-sided games rather than the full-sided games?

Mickey did his PhD with me. He worked very hard.

What was funny... he was down in the graduate room with all the other graduate students. And they were all doing physiology and genetics and all of that. But Mickey barely knew how to switch on a computer! It was so funny, but the environment it created! He became a father figure.

Those kids absolutely adored him. They absolutely loved him.

The reason was… he got to know every one of them.

They were with him every single day, and they know the impact he had on their lives. He shared his knowledge, his experience, and they were prepared to give up their time, because he was so good to them all. He would bring them out for dinner around Christmastime; he never forgot their birthdays, people don't realise that side of Mickey at all.

They would help him use excel and stuff.

But Mickey was old school.

We put everything into excel, and the students would show him how to do all the calculations in two seconds. What would Mickey do? He would arrive with the excel, the software, and he would arrive with this big folder. He would have everything done in pencil as well. Everything!

And if there was a number missing, Mickey would go home and he would spend eight hours correcting it. From a statistical perspective, I would tell him, 'It's not going to make any materialistic difference'.

No, Mickey had to be one hundred percent right. He had that old school aspect, he was methodical in every single thing that he did.

Imagine being in your late-sixties or early-seventies, having not been in college for years, and all of a sudden you are in the era of computers and PDFs and there were journals here, there and everywhere.

There were times Mickey just wasn't happy with the degree of progress, and he'd come into my office and say, 'Ah Niall, maybe I should give it up'.

I'd retort, 'Maybe you should… maybe it's a bit beyond you!'

All of a sudden, away he'd go more determined than ever! We have a phenomenal relationship.

I used to just sit back in awe of the man who in his late-sixties still had this thirst for knowledge. And not just the knowledge to affirm what he knew, but then to be able to take that information and to take it to the nation.

One of the greatest legacies that Mickey will leave, and people don't really appreciate this… Mickey's PhD was really the genesis of the Go Games.

When we went around the country presenting it, that was the evidence that we presented. You have to be an idiot to disagree!

With his colleague and friend Niall Moyna (they are either side of GAA President John Horan) when the association launched LCPE.ie in 2018. And (bottom of page) being honoured to host a Legends Tour in Croke Park.

- Lifetime in sport
- Parents coaches teachers
- Playing experiences

Mickey enjoys passing on everything he has learned (above at the GAA Games Development Conference in 2018).

« CHAPTER 17 »

NIALL MOYNA INVITED Mickey to work with the DCU senior football team during his stint as a part-time lecturer at the university.

They went close in his first year involved, losing the Sigerson Cup semi-final in 2005. They came back stronger the following year.

Niall was worried one day about the team, scratching his head wondering if they had what it takes. 'Listen, there's the makings of a team that's going to win the All-Ireland there!' Mickey told him. It was a talented group. They did go further in 2006, and won the Sigerson Cup for the first time in DCU's history.

There were some key figures in Dublin's 2011 All-Ireland winning team involved with DCU that year. Stephen Cluxton was in goals. Bryan Cullen was involved, while Bernard Brogan also lined out.

There was talent from around the country across to the team too, including Mayo's Conor Mortimer and Cavan's Seanie Johnston.

DCU sealed the title with a 0-11 to 1-4 final win over Queen's at Parnell Park.

After that Mickey decided to step away.

'I tend to step aside when we achieve our goal, and only when I am confident my younger colleagues are ready to continue the progress achieved.

'But working with Niall on the sideline, and not only in an academic setting, was brilliant. I made sure it was not the last time we collaborated on a successful coaching project.

NIALL MOYNA

I invited Mickey into the DCU coaching team and he had an immediate impact. We won our first ever Sigerson Cup in 2006. Once you have Mickey Whelan close by you, you can't go far wrong! Mickey's input that year was absolutely phenomenal.

Without a doubt, Mickey getting to work with some of those Dublin players on the DCU team helped the county team when he took over alongside Pat Gilroy. That whole link certainly played a role. It was one of many parts of a big jigsaw. But it was nonetheless an important part.

You only have to be around Mickey just to see his impact. It was Kevin Heffernan one day who said to me in the bar in Vincent's… 'You cannot coach or teach what Mickey Whelan has… because he sees games through the lens that very few other people can see!'

◄◄◆►►

THE 2006 SIGERSON Cup was not Mickey's first rodeo when it came to coaching in third level sport. Far from it, in fact. Down through the years, he managed numerous DIT teams through gaelic football, hurling and indeed soccer. As soon as he took up his post in DIT, he got involved in the college's sporting teams.

Nowadays, the Trench Cup is a second-tier tournament below the Sigerson Cup. Originally however, it was a tournament for non-university colleges.

Mickey helped DIT to the Trench Cup title for the first time in 1987.

'We had a brilliant team… Christy Grogan, Cian Long, Seanie McEniff, Mick Egan and Fergus Rowley to name just a few.

'That year, my son Cormac was playing with DCU.

'Cormac was a very good footballer, and could have made it. He was one of the key players on the DCU team.' Mickey knew his son's strengths.

Before the match started, he gave the DIT team clear instructions.

'Listen lads, I've seen these guys play a bit. They have a very good midfielder. He's a very tall guy, an excellent fielder who sets up most of their attacks. We need to be smart on our kick out. Kick the ball to the opposite side to where he positions himself… and our marking midfielder, position yourself alongside and between him and the ball Force him to go round you, make it very difficult for him to get at our kick outs. On their kick outs, our two midfielders mark the big guy. The half-forward drops back to mark their free midfielder on his side.

'DIT won the game.

'As we were gathering on the pitch to decide how and where we were going to celebrate our win, I heard the words… "Hey dad… you had those guys wired!"

'Cormac knew I had made special arrangements for him to be tightly marked.

'Some of the DIT players took umbrage at that. They thought him calling me *Dad* was a throwaway ageist remark and were heading to confront him.

'I told them to relax.

'They were angry. I told them, "He's my son".

'They were astonished. Cormac and I were well able to park it.

'What happened on the pitch, stayed on the pitch!'

MICKEY GUIDED DIT to Trench Cup victories in 1995 and '97 as well. They also won a Ryan Cup, hurling's second tier below the Fitzgibbon Cup, in 1994.

This was around the time that he was coaching Dundalk and then managing the Dublin footballers. 'It was not too hard a balancing act. The beauty of third level sport is that training and matches are often midweek. Dundalk and then Dublin training would be in the evenings with matches at the weekend.

He also managed DIT win two national soccer championships around that time, in the Irish Technical Colleges Football Association competitions.

As an Institute of Technology, they were not allowed into the Collingwood Cup at the time, which was reserved for the country's universities. They eventually knocked hard enough on the door that they were allowed in, and more than justified their admission by reaching the final in 2001.

They were denied the trophy by Jordanstown, who beat them by a single goal in the decider.

IN 1991 MICKEY first got involved with the Irish universities soccer team, heading to Sheffield for the World University Games, otherwise known as The Universiade.

Ireland, for the first time, entered men's and women's soccer teams in the games. The teams were packed with talented players from universities across the island of Ireland – Mickey was selected as coach for the men's team, working with fellow coach Kieran Dowd and manager Alex McKee. Both men were prominent athletes in their younger years and, on retirement, each went on to achieve eminence in sports management.

Alex McKee, who died after a short illness in 2020 at the age of 81, grew up on a farm at the foot of Slemish Mountain in Antrim and working on that farm helped build a strong young man, who, when he entered Stranmillis Teacher Training College was ready to take on all sports. He excelled at rugby and basketball, amongst other sports, though soccer became his number one game. Moving to Ballymena to teach, he soon became a regular for Ballymena United with whom he made 90 appearances. He managed the team for four years as well.

'It was a brilliant experience to work alongside Alex McKee, the team manager… a thorough gentleman and a brilliant coach, who led his beloved Ballymena United to victory two years previously in the 1989 Irish Cup Final.

'Kieran Dowd was an accomplished soccer player too. He signed for his local club Cliftonville when he was just 16, and made his debut one year later. He was Director of Physical Education and Sport in University College Cork, and in 1984 and '85 was at the helm when UCC unluckily lost consecutive Collingwood Cup finals. However, over several decades, many hundreds of students who attended the college were indebted to him for his knowledge and service. He was first chair of the Colleges and Universities Sports Association (CUSAI). He also saw the safe delivery of the Mardyke Arena.

'He worked with so many exceptional athletes… rugby legends like Donal Lenihan and Moss Keane, and footballers like Seamus Moynihan and Maurice Fitzgerald and Anthony Lynch. Frank Lohan and Nicky English and Joe Deane benefited from Kieran's excellence in his role in the college, and so too did athletes in so many sports. The hockey star Mary Logue, athletes like Billy Oakes and Ray Shanahan, and camogie stars like Stephanie Dunlea and Una O'Dwyer.'

Kieran Dowd was from the same part of the country as Alex, and it was with these two men from the north-east that Mickey quickly developed a brilliant working relationship, and friendship that endured long after their time working together.

'I was very pleased to join two outstanding coaches, who accepted me into their management team as an assistant coach at a worldwide international sporting event. We had numerous trial games in different parts of the country, and when we settled on the squad to travel we moved to weekend training sessions. The real positive outcome for me was that Kieran, Alex and myself became lifelong friends. World University Games is similar to the Olympics for third level students. Many student games competitors go on to achieve Olympian standards in their sport.

'I was immediately hooked.

'We were coming up against countries with differing styles of play. We did not know what to expect from them. So we set about informing ourselves regarding which teams were in our group… when we were playing them, what times… and where they were booked for practice and training.

'Most of the footballers involved would go on to have professional careers.'

The event takes place every second year, and Mickey went on to manage various soccer teams before he was honoured with the role of Head Of Delegation.

'It was a massive learning experience. It broadened my horizons.

'I travelled to many different countries to attend the World University Games. They would take place in huge stadia, in front of massive crowds. I was acquiring incredible experience, meeting many bright, friendly people from a wide variety of sports. Needless to say, I was not shy about asking questions if I thought I might learn something.

'I also relished getting up early in the morning, and just walking around to watch athletes and teams go through warm-ups or training sessions. It was fascinating to see what various countries were doing differently.

'I was struck with how the Japanese would go about their business. They were always hard at it, and always did well in their respective sports. I would observe drills, and think how I could apply some of those principles to GAA or soccer training.

'There were small things I would pick up, write down and memorise to throw into a training session at a later date.

'The more ways you can learn to do things in different instances, the better. Using different tweaks will prevent teams growing bored of repetition. What struck me as well was how open coaches from all over the world were to idea-sharing. Each day there were meetings for all the coaches and the heads of delegations. Most evenings, a few coaches from the various English-speaking countries would go out together for a few beers, a tea or coffee and a chat. There was a great camaraderie. We discussed the day's successful and unsuccessful experiences.

'One year, I was joined on the trip to China by Brian Mullins, who was there in his capacity as a member of the management team.

'As two St Vincent's men, we were a long way from Marino!'

◄◄◆►►

BRIAN MULLINS

Mickey and I ended up at the World University Games together in Beijing in 2001.

He was always learning from other sports. He always understood the importance of looking at the crossover in different sports.

If you were to go back through Mickey's whole history, he has been involved in not only gaelic football and hurling teams and now camogie teams, but soccer teams too. I don't think there has ever been a period when he was not coaching – even when he was in DCU doing his PhD in his seventies, he was involved in teams there and sports there.

◄◄◆►►

'IN 2005, I was reappointed Chef de Mission, for the third time for an event in Izmir, Turkey.

'Derval O'Rourke competed that year, winning bronze in the 100m hurdles. Ailis McSweeney – who later married Bryan Cullen – got silver in the 100m race.

'The two combined on the 4x100m relay team to take bronze.

'Paul Hession took bronze in the 200m.

'That year, we brought home one silver and seven bronze medals… a haul which still stands as a record for an Irish delegation at the Games.

'Over the years, I never found any massive differences in dealing with athletes in different sports… be it gaelic football, hurling, camogie, soccer, athletics or anything else. At the end of the day, athletes are people and that is who you are dealing with.

'When we attend or watch the World University Games, we are seeing many future greats. It is the pinnacle of third level sport, and I was blessed and thankful to be involved.'

With Brian Mullins, his former teammate, at the World University Games in China (above) and with a selection of the Irish participants.

爱尔兰
Ireland

It was a great honour for him to represent Ireland at the games, and get to work with such valued colleagues.

« EPILOGUE »

'WHAT'S NEXT?

'I don't know… honestly.

'But I will keep on, keeping on.

'And I aim to keep busy until that day when, God willing, I will meet my beloved Irene again.

'I left Sutton Park in 2015, and moved to Fairview where I now live… close to St Vincent's GAA club and Croke Park.'

'IN OCTOBER OF 2018, Germaine Noonan, the manager of the St Vincent's senior camogie team, invited me to join their management team.

'I enquired who else was on the management team, and the response was Patsy Hetherton.

'I was in!

'These two women had played together on winning Dublin Club Championship teams, and Leinster Club Championship winning teams, and were very unlucky to lose an All-Ireland final to Granagh-Ballingarry in 1998. They also played together on Dublin senior county teams for years.

'Germaine also won a senior All-Ireland medal with Dublin in 1984. The last Dublin team to win the O'Duffy Cup.

'I joined the camogie team in 2018, and we were beaten by Ballyboden St

Enda's in the semi-final. In 2019, we won the Dublin League and Championship, and went on to beat St Martin's of Wexford in a replay to win the Leinster Club Championship. The first time for a Dublin club to do so since Ballyboden St Enda's win in 2008.

'St Vincent's were beaten in the All-Ireland semi-final by an excellent Galway Sarsfields team, who went on to become All-Ireland champions.

'In 2020, we won the first three matches and then the league competition was discontinued due to the Covid-19 pandemic. The Championship was resurrected later in a truncated season and St Jude's defeated us in the final.

'I am entering the fourth year of my first involvement with a camogie team, and I am really enjoying the journey.'

'RETURNING TO THE training field following the Covid lockdowns was a massively welcome boost. I am very fortunate to be a part of such a great management team and a terrific group of talented camogie players.

'There is also a new addition to our camogie backroom team.

'In May of 2021, I encouraged Pat Gilroy to join us.

'We're together again.

'And it's brilliant to be back planning training sessions, getting out early to lay out the cones… and chat to people afterwards in the club.

'It's great to be back.'

◄◄◆►►

PAT GILROY

I would have known Mickey from when I was really small.

He would have been in and out of the house with my father. I can remember him being in the house when I was five or six. Between himself and Heffo, they would have been the ones regularly there… talking about whatever they were talking about.

They were close with my dad.

Mickey and I are back coaching together, working with the St Vincent's camogie team. They're a great bunch of girls. He won a championship with them two years ago, and they went on to win a Leinster championship, but lost an All-Ireland semi-final. They were beaten in the final last year.

There's a lot of young players... my own daughter is playing. I had never managed her. I managed all the other kids that I have... coaching and stuff, but I had never done anything with her team.

So I'm glad to be back working with Mickey.

Great craic!

Although he is the manager, no matter what way we have done things down through the years, once we do something together, there's no... 'He's in charge... or I'm in charge!'

There's never been a time when we didn't eventually agree on a decision between the two of us. We never had to talk about whose role was what.

We just get on with things.

He can pick up the slack with me, and I can pick up the slack with him. We're very much in sync... we don't have to bother with too much formality.

He has never lost that thirst for coaching. You see him now with the camogie team... he's now 82, and he's right in the middle of the training... how to hit the ball, how to get your balance right.

He's incredibly fit for a man of his age.

He has the fitness of a 50-year-old. He keeps himself in great nick.

And he's showing no signs of stopping!

◄◄◆►►

'IRENE WAS THE best thing that ever happened to me.

'I've said that once already in this book, and I will say it all my life. She was my strength.

'Irene imbued me with confidence from the first night we met as teenagers two months before her 17th birthday and two months before my 18th birthday.

'My beloved Irene passed away nine years ago, but there is not a day goes by that I do not think of her... confident, attractive, gentle and fun-loving.

'Irene passed away on March 9, 2013.

'I can't even begin to describe how much I miss her.'

Irene and Mickey with the Sam Maguire Cup in 1963, and the happy couple after their wedding two years later.